LYNNE M. BAAB

BEATING BURNOUT
IN CONGREGATIONS

FOREWORD BY

ROY M. OSWALD

The Alban Institute

Myers-Briggs Type Indicator and MBTI are registered trademarks of Consulting Psychologists Press, Palo Alto, California.

Grateful acknowledgment is expressed to *Perspectives* magazine for permission to quote extensively from "Ministry Is Exhaustion" by Virginia Wiles (January 2002).

Scripture quotations, unless otherwise noted, are from the New Revised Standard Version of the Bible, copyright © 1989, Division of Christian Education of the National Council of the Churches of Christ in the United States of American and are used by permission.

CONTENTS

Congregations today are continually under siege. We are experiencing increasing attacks from outside congregations as we move more deeply into a post-Christendom or postmodern era. Whereas in the early 1960s and 1970s we felt as though we were living in a friendly environment, as we move into the twenty-first century the environment is sometimes friendly and sometimes hostile. Congregations are no longer welcomed in neighborhoods as consistently as they were in past decades. Congregations are also under siege from the inside, however. Internal forces—most recently, clergy sexual scandals—are splitting congregations apart and taking their toll on congregational health.

In this excellently written book, Lynne Baab describes another devastating way in which congregations are doing themselves in. Congregational burnout is an inside job, and this malady can literally suck the life out of a healthy congregation.

For years I have been focusing much energy on clergy burnout. For the past 15 years, I have led workshops to help clergy avoid the devastation of burnout. The number of requests for workshops on this subject has outstripped the requests for any other type of workshop I offer. Whenever I am in front of a group of clergy I can assume at least twenty percent of them are experiencing severe burnout, with another twenty percent already suffering some of the symptoms and perhaps bordering on burnout.

What I find saddest about the phenomenon of burnout is that it afflicts our most committed people, both clergy and lay leaders. Burnout has often been called a disease of the overcommitted. When normal people feel exhausted or depleted, they take note of this and back off to give themselves space and rest. Overcommitted people don't do that. Even when they are totally drained, they continue to try to give more. Their level of commitment to their task won't allow them to do anything else.

Congregations, however, do not have in place systems for monitoring whether a particular volunteer is overextended and becoming increasingly exhausted, cynical, and self-deprecating. As a result of burnout, I believe, we are losing some of our most committed lay leaders out the back door. Now is clearly the time for a book on the burnout of congregational volunteers.

Although there are many definitions of burnout, most social scientists agree on these four characteristics:

- physical and emotional exhaustion
- cynicism
- disillusionment
- self-deprecation.

These characteristics hardly describe an effective agent of good news! Burned-out people can talk about their faith experience, but everything else about them communicates a different message. The symptoms of burnout are all too obvious, and burned-out people can neither authentically nor credibly share the good news of their relationship with God. The recipient of such a mixed message might well say to herself, "If this good news means I'll become like you, I'm not interested!"

What I find in my own experience of dealing with burned-out volunteers is that many of them begin to lose respect for fellow congregants. Volunteers who burn out usually have fairly responsible roles—they are leaders—and need to depend on other members of the congregation to get their job done. When these other members do not fulfill their responsibility according to leaders' expectations, these burned-out volunteers simply lose respect for them.

In addition, burned-out lay leaders often lose their ability to worship. Before worship begins, people remind them of things that need to be accomplished. When they finally do get to sit in the pew in silence, they look around the congregation and notice all the other people who seem not to take their volunteer roles "seriously enough." After worship, leaders often need to field questions, check on plans for upcoming activities, run a stand-up meeting, host a congregational event, or tend to some other task that might keep them from going home until midafternoon.

Burned-out volunteers also often loose respect for their clergyperson. Because of their role, they often spend long hours in meetings with their pastor and get to see that she or he is all too human and sometimes does not respond well under pressure, something the majority of congregants never witness. Often-present leaders become increasingly disillusioned with their pastor, and when their term of office is complete or they finally work up the courage to resign from a task, these lay leaders sneak out the back door of the church and join the congregation's inactive roll.

This book should receive your attention, not only because it describes burnout within congregations through a great variety of individual stories, but because it offers strategies for addressing this affliction. I am particularly enthused by Baab's emphasis on the need for congregations to pay attention to members' motivated gifts and experience of God's call to specific tasks. People don't burn out when they feel their gifts are being used well.

For me, the key to preventing burnout among congregational volunteers is to ensure that volunteers who accept any task receive some clear benefit, one that fits their personal motivations for ministry. Achievement types are motivated by the invitation to take on a tough challenge. Affiliation types like to work alongside other people. I am highly motivated by opportunities to learn something new or to address an issue for which I have great passion.

The challenge, however, is finding ways to assess where congregational members are motivated to contribute their gifts. Some congregations hire professionals who help members determine what role would contribute meaning to their lives. Here Lynne Baab offers another gift in this book. She outlines ways individuals or task forces might use typology to assist them in placing volunteers in roles that help them feel valued and well used within their congregation. The Myers-Briggs Type Indicator and the Enneagram are two well-grounded theories that can help congregations assess where members will experience the greatest satisfaction in ministry. I have a great fondness for both these instruments and was delighted when I encountered Baab's solid use of them in this book.

Beating Burnout in Congregations makes a real contribution to one of the maladies that can torpedo congregational health from the inside. As we remain vigilant about the many ways that congregations are under siege, both outside and inside their walls, we clearly need to watch carefully that burnout does not destroy our congregations from the inside. When congregation leaders and other volunteers burn out, we must surely believe that this is not what God has in mind for us. This book will help readers reassess God's call to service, so that those who do offer their skill, knowledge, and energy become uplifted, healthier, and stronger. Congregational leaders would do well to take this book seriously.

ROY M. OSWALD

I became interested in burnout among church members while doing interviews for the two books I wrote about midlife. Lots of people talked to me about burnout as a significant part of their midlife experience. Often they did not use the word *burnout*, but they described the way they had pursued something until their energy and enthusiasm were depleted.

I was struck during the interviews that this process of depletion was often the beginning of a fresh start. Many people told me that their lack of energy for the things that used to interest them stimulated a healthy process of reevaluation. They asked a lot of questions about what they really should be doing, what they really wanted to do. They began to examine their lives to find out what energized rather than drained them. All in all, it seemed to me as I listened to people talk, burnout often led to life-giving changes. Admittedly, those changes often came after a long period that was unpleasant and disorienting, but the end result was often something lovely.

I also heard some individuals talk about intensely disturbing experiences at midlife that could only be called a midlife crisis. According to a MacArthur Foundation study published in 1999, only about 10 percent of people experience a true midlife crisis. This figure fit with my anecdotal data. I talked with more than a hundred people about their midlife experiences, and only about a dozen had gone through the intense questioning and upheaval that we recognize as a midlife crisis.

I began to see a midlife crisis, in the small number who experience it, as a form of burnout. All those questions and doubts and discouragement come from being burned out on life in general. Most of the people who talked to me about these kinds of intense experiences at midlife came out on the other side refreshed—often some years later—with a renewed sense of vision.

As we begin this study of burnout in congregations, I want to make clear two principles that underlie everything I have written in this book. First, I do believe that congregational leaders should do everything they can to help congregation members find healthy places to serve, places where people can make a significant contribution using their gifts and abilities and where they can experience joy and fulfillment. In other words, as you will see, I do believe congregations should do everything possible to create an environment that does not encourage burnout.

But, at the same time, I believe that although we can avoid burnout by discovering and using our gifts well, burnout itself can be a gift. I cannot tell you how many people told me that their experience of burnout led them to make significant changes that have proved to be healthy and life-giving. We must not fear burnout; instead, we need to do a better job coming alongside people as they experience burnout, and help them figure out what they are learning.

The Scope of This Book

This is a book about burnout in congregations. We will touch briefly here and there on burnout among ordained ministers and rabbis, but the main focus of the book will be on congregation members as they experience burnout in their volunteer positions in their churches and synagogues and, to a lesser extent, in their work. A second occasional focus will be the nonclergy support staff in congregations. Staff members in congregations are often stretched to serve in ways that cause exhaustion and discouragement.

One of the ironies of the study of burnout is the lack of a precise definition. We use the word frequently in conversation in a variety of ways. "I burned out on teaching Sunday school so I'm taking a break now." "I've been trying to eat a healthier diet, and I'm burning out on carrots and celery." "I'm getting burned out listening to my wife talk about the conflict she's experiencing at work."

In the early chapters of the book, we will look at a variety of definitions of burnout. Before we look at those definitions, I do want to point out the range of burnout experiences. On one end of the spectrum is an all-encompassing kind of burnout where one's entire life is affected. This kind of burnout happens most often in the workplace. One social worker said that after job burnout it took her a full year before she had any energy at all.

At the other end of the spectrum is burnout in a very specific and usually small part of our lives, such as the person who is burned out on eating carrots and celery. It may take a year before that person enjoys carrots again, but this kind of narrow and limited burnout does not overflow into all areas of life.

Burnout among congregation volunteers usually falls somewhere in the middle of this spectrum. Most people who experience burnout because of preparing coffee every week or teaching Sunday school for too long will not be totally exhausted in every part of their lives. But neither will their burnout be as localized to just one part of their life, as in the case of the person who has eaten too many crunchy vegetables. Sadly, for most people, burnout from too much serving in their congregation raises significant questions about God. In addition, because volunteers who burn out often leave their congregation for a while, volunteer burnout can keep us from participating in the very patterns of faith observance that have comforted us in the past and helped us feel close to God. Burnout's repercussions for the spiritual life of individuals are the most significant burnout-related issue in congregations.

The Irony of Congregational Burnout

The world is a broken and often painful place, with great needs that sometimes seem overwhelming. Sometimes our own brokenness feels overwhelming, too, and we know that we need healing and love. We long to experience transcendence in the midst of the challenges and complexities of daily life in our frantic culture. We desire love, peace, joy, wholeness, and well-being.

While no faith community can completely meet these needs, people do look to their congregations, hoping to find these longings taken seriously. Recently in my Presbyterian congregation, the board was discussing a controversial policy change. Congregational forums were planned, so the congregation could ask questions and give input on the difficult topic. One of my friends said to me, "My life is so chaotic and wearisome. I need my church to be a place of nurture and peace. I can't bear the thought of attending a forum in order to hear people disagree with each other." Her desire for her church to be a place different from the world, an oasis in a desert, is not unusual.

In addition, often our view of God is intricately intertwined with our experience in our congregation. When hurtful and disturbing things happen in our congregation, we wonder how God could let that happen. In fact, we may find it hard to continue to have faith and trust in God when things are not going well in the congregation.

These are the reasons why burnout among volunteers and staff in a congregation carries so much weight. The congregation is a place where people expect to find life and health and healing. If a person—or many people—experience exhaustion, discouragement, and pain in the very place that promised to give life, then what does that say about our faith? Our values? God? I can only shake my head in the face of the irony that all too often the very place where we look for life and health, the very place where we expect to nurture and deepen a loving relationship with God, can cause so many to experience the exact opposite.

Life in the Fast Lane

We will see in this book that some congregational burnout is caused by the structures and culture of the congregation itself, some is caused by forces at work within the individual, and some burnout is caused by a combination of both. Sometimes stresses in the congregation are simply the last straw for a person who is experiencing stress in many areas of life. Whatever the root causes of burnout, the whole process is played out against a backdrop of the "hurry sickness" of our culture.

Everything is moving faster, it seems. Recently an article in our local newspaper talked about the fast pace of life for children these days. The article was entitled "Children in the Fast Lane," and I could feel myself getting tired just reading about the schedules kept by many of the children and teens featured in the article.

The adults and children and youth who come to our congregations do need an oasis of peace in the midst of the horrendous pace most of them keep. Yet we must do significant work in order to maintain these oases. Someone has to see that the building is kept up. Someone needs to serve coffee and food to provide opportunities to be together and talk and make friends in a relaxed atmosphere. Someone needs to oversee the prayer retreats and learning opportunities that help people center their lives in God in the midst of all the fragmentation of daily life. Someone needs to run the sound system and perform the music and collect the offering so that the congregation can find peace through worship.

This is the second irony of congregational burnout. The very place that provides refuge in the insane pace of our hurried daily life has to encourage its volunteers to keep moving and keep busy in order for the congregation to function. How can that be healthy?

At the same time that we ponder this irony, we also must acknowledge that many congregational volunteers find meaning and life in their service that they do not find elsewhere. My husband works half time and spends much of the rest of his time volunteering at church and at an inner-city mission. In our most recent Christmas letter, he reflected to friends that his volunteer work is so much more satisfying than his paid work. He gets a sense of meaning from his volunteering that he does not get at work; he feels he is helping people who would not otherwise receive that help. For him, being helpful is a way he experiences God's presence in his life. He has stepped out of life in the career fast lane in order to serve and give, and he is experiencing great joy.

So, for some volunteers, their unpaid service is life-giving. For others, their serving is one more frantic commitment that keeps them rushing in the fast lane and robs them of the life and joy they might otherwise receive in their congregation. What makes the difference? That's part of what we will explore in this book.

Holy Moments

Service can be life-giving for many congregation members because somehow they encounter God there. Rabbi Abraham Heschel, in his lovely book on the Sabbath, writes that the purpose of spiritual living is to recognize holy moments.[1] This requires an ability to stop and notice, to take time to reflect on the events of the day in order to see God's hand and God's presence.

How can we recognize those holy moments if we are moving so fast that life passes by us in a blur? How can we perceive God's presence in time if our highest priority is accomplishing things?

At a recent church gathering, one woman described a holy moment. Tina works full time and has three school-age children. Her mornings are frantic and stressful: fixing breakfast for her husband and kids, preparing five lunches, cleaning up the kitchen, getting organized for dinner so she can throw it quickly together after work, and starting a load of laundry.

One morning the low winter sun shone into the window above her sink just as she was washing dishes. Clouds were clustered near the sun and they glowed with brilliant color. Rays of sunlight poured down from the sun. Tina stopped what she was doing—for a few seconds, anyway—and just looked. God seemed to be telling her that God is shining into her life just like that sunlight shines into her window. She held onto that moment all day.

Our congregations are full of people like Tina whose mornings and days and evenings are packed so full of activities that they often feel they do not have time to breathe. We need to help them learn to take the time to watch for those holy moments. Some of our parishioners will experience those holy moments as they serve in the congregation. And some of them will be robbed of the ability to experience those holy moments because of the exhaustion caused by too much serving.

As we discuss burnout in congregations, we have to hold in tension three truths:

1. Many of the people in many of our congregations are infected with the "hurry sickness" that is epidemic in Western culture in the early 21st century. They need their congregations to be places of refuge where they can find rest and refreshment. They need their congregations to encourage them to find a healthier rhythm as they live in time, and they need encouragement to notice holy moments.

2. In order for congregations to be places of rest and refreshment, lots of things have to be done by lots of people. Congregations depend on volunteers in order to fulfill their holy purpose. So we simply cannot say that we want our congregations to be oases of peace where no one has to do anything productive, and everyone can experience rest and relaxation all the time. We need volunteers to enable the congregation to be what it is designed to be.

3. Some people will find joy, satisfaction, and meaning in their service in their congregation. They will experience holy moments as they serve. Their service will actually have aspects that are refreshing to them. Others will be pushed by their serving to a place that is not healthy or life-giving, and their negative experience will probably spill over into their life of faith outside the congregation as well.

In this book we will explore what leaders can do to help make their congregations healthy places to serve. We will look at burnout from lots of different angles to try to get a handle on its causes and cures. We will try our best to try to understand how to prevent burnout. But we will also remember that some burnout seems to be inevitable. One mark of a healthy congregation is that people are encouraged to rejoice that God can work in their lives in all situations, including burnout. Indeed, burnout can enable us to reshape our priorities and have a fresh start. We can learn valuable lessons from burnout that we would not learn anywhere else.

My Hopes for This Book

You will see stories throughout this book, both in boxes and in the body of the text. As I researched this book, I heard many different stories about what burnout looks like. The stories shaped my understanding of burnout, and I believe they will help you gain a stronger sense of the many faces of burnout in congregations. I hope the stories will round out your understanding of burnout and give you an intuitive sense of what burnout looks like in congregations. I have changed the names and some of the identifying details in the stories. Occasionally a story is a composite of what two or three people told me.

Throughout the book I refer to "congregational leaders" and the ways they are called to care for members of the congregation so that burnout can be avoided as much as possible. In using the words "congregational leaders," I am thinking about ordained ministers and rabbis. I am thinking about board members who are charged with the spiritual oversight of the congregation. I am also thinking about committee chairs and anyone in a congregation who recruits people for volunteer positions: the nursery coordinator, the person or people who recruit the teachers for children and youth, the person who organizes the coffee hour and the helpers for dinners and social events, the people who recruit teachers for adult classes. It is not just the ordained ministers and rabbis who are congregational leaders. It is not only the clergy who should be asking volunteers, "How are you doing? Are you experiencing joy in your serving?" All congregational leaders—lay or ordained—are responsible, to a greater or lesser degree, for the spiritual care of the volunteers who serve in their area.

My hope and prayer for this book is that our congregations will become healthier places to serve because we understand burnout better. We all know that life is getting more complex and increasingly frantic. We know that our congregation members face challenges and complexities in their work and at home that were unimaginable a couple of generations ago. I pray that this book will help congregational leaders in their own lives as they seek to serve God with dedication and devotion. And I pray that, because of this book, congregational leaders will be more equipped to nurture the entire congregation into patterns of healthy and life-giving service.

ACKNOWLEDGMENTS

My thoughts about burnout in congregations were greatly influenced by the many people who took time to talk to me. In many cases, I picked up a vivid and helpful tidbit from an informal conversation; other times, I conducted formal interviews. I am grateful to everyone who talked to me about burnout, including Dale Brandenstein, Sr. Joyce Cox, the Rev. Kim Crispeno, Linda Cutshall, Rabbi Dan Danson, the Rev. Amy Delaney, the Rev. Julie Denny-Hughes, the Rev. Monica Elvig, Dr. Rich Erickson, Susan Forshey, Paul Foster, Ann Hammond, Betty Heutink, Kathy Hooper, the Rev. Francis Horner, Carol Jordan, Cecily Kaplan, Jane Kise, the Rev. Mark Labberton, the Rev. Dick Leon, Dianne Long, Laura MacMillan, Dr. Nancy Bost Millner, John Morford, Randy Mumaw, Loretta Pain, Greg and Amy Pang, the Rev. Jane Plantinga Pauw, the Rev. Allan Poole, Dianne Ross, the Rev. Lee Seese, Rabbi Beth Singer, Dr. Walter Smith, Jenny Sugiyama, the Rev. Deb Sunoo, Rabbi Daniel Weiner, and Jeanette Yep.

In 2000 and 2001, I taught daylong seminars on burnout and personality type four times for the Center for Applications of Psychological Type and once at the international conference of the Association for Psychological Type. I am grateful for the participants in those seminars who told me many interesting stories and shaped my understanding of burnout both in the workplace and in congregations.

I am indebted to the Rev. Kim Crispeno and Anne Baumgartner for explaining many things about the Enneagram and for suggesting books that helped me deepen my understanding of Enneagram type.

This is the third book I have worked on with Beth Gaede, my editor at the Alban Institute. I am grateful for her encouragement, her wisdom about church matters, and the way she helps me improve my writing.

Four people gave valuable time to read the manuscript. I am grateful to Anne Baumgartner, Brian Ives, and Lori Reimann, who made many helpful suggestions. The fourth generous reader was my husband, Dave Baab, who partners with me as I strive to serve God in the healthy ways described in this book.

1
INTRODUCTION TO BURNOUT

Burnout
1. A state of emotional exhaustion caused by the stresses of one's work or responsibilities.[1]
2. The body's doing the work, but the spirit's not present.[2]

If I had to pick out one story of burnout in a congregation most typical of what I have heard, I would tell you Pam's story.

After serving a year on the fellowship committee in her church, she agreed to chair the committee. She was full of enthusiasm, vision, and ideas. The fellowship committee in her congregation is very active, overseeing coffee hour every week, serving a monthly dinner open to the congregation, and sponsoring several other special events each year.

During the year Pam had served on the committee, she watched the committee members struggle to stay on top of the workload and strain to get volunteers to help with all the events. She came into the role of committee chair with a strong desire to provide support and encouragement to the committee members.

Pam began a new plan for the monthly committee meetings. Formerly, the meetings had centered around all the tasks that needed to be done. Pam introduced a significant time devoted to Bible study and prayer at each meeting. She felt that focusing on business for two hours was draining, and she herself experienced Bible study and prayer to be restoring, so she figured the committee members would find energy if they studied and prayed together. Pam really enjoyed designing these study and prayer times, and sometimes they got quite lengthy. Once or twice they took up three-quarters of the meeting time. The committee's business—dividing up tasks for immediate events and looking ahead to future events—had to be squeezed into the remaining short time.

The members of the committee were uncomfortable with the new structure. They would not have minded 15 minutes of devotions, but they felt Pam's extravagant and creative study and prayer experiences left too little time to accomplish the essential tasks of the committee. None of the committee members were comfortable with conflict. They all had the quiet gift of service, and they were more at ease doing things than talking about them. So they said nothing to Pam, hoping they could endure until she was finished with her year as chairperson.

Despite the committee members' attempts to be polite and submissive, Pam was affected by the withdrawal of their support and encouragement. She could not really put her finger on it, but after every committee meeting, she felt let down and dissatisfied.

The year wore on, and she became more and more discouraged without knowing why. Her energy for giving support to the committee members faded away. Her enthusiasm for the congregational fellowship events drained away as well. At the end of her year as committee chair, she stopped attending church entirely. After a few months, she sat in the pew at another church from time to time. It was 18 months before she could think about returning to her church without feeling heaviness and pain just from imagining being there.

Unlike many people who experience burnout, Pam never really figured out why she grew to be so uncomfortable in her role of committee chair. She did learn enough to know that when she returned to church, she would avoid anything related to coffee hours and church dinners.

Six Pictures of Burnout in Congregations

As I interviewed people from synagogues and churches, large and small, I heard many tales of burnout. I want to give you a flavor of the kind of stories I heard so you can get a beginning sense of where and why burnout occurs. Here are six pictures of burnout in diverse congregations.

A congregation with frequent clergy turnover.

Susan, the pastor of a small Presbyterian church, says:

> When I came to the church four years ago, I could tell the whole congregation was experiencing some degree of burnout. Every time I would present a new idea, even if it was a pretty small and insignificant suggestion, there was simply

no interest. I had started out new at other churches before, and I knew this was more than the normal mild resistance to a new pastor.

Then I thought back on the past decade in this congregation. Their last installed pastor was going through a difficult divorce in his last years in the congregation. Then they had an interim pastor for two years. He had been asked to leave his previous church. He was struggling with his sense of identity and wondering if he would ever get another job in a church. His concerns were valid. When he finished the interim, he was unable to get another church position and he ultimately went into another line of work. The congregation, and particularly its leaders, wished they could have done more to help those two men, and their pain and sadness paralyzed and exhausted them. They needed rest from turmoil and pain, and mercifully my personal life has been relatively calm since my arrival. Nothing traumatic has happened in the congregation, either, and they have been able to get the emotional rest they needed. Now, four years after the last interim left and I arrived on the scene, I am happy to report that they seem enthusiastic and healthy again.

A very active congregation with high standards and lots of programs.

Listen to David talk about his congregation, a small church with a deep commitment to social action and lots of social programs.

This congregation is prone to burnout. This is a group of high achievers. They want to do so many things, and they can do them well. They have high standards in every area of life. They just cannot do a mediocre job. They love to say, "Look at what this little congregation is doing!"

Their orientation is to be doers and workers. You do, do, do for the Lord. Worship, personal piety, meditation are not big words in this church. But the soup kitchen is big. People love to come here because there is a lot going on. If a person loves the social gospel, they thrive here but they are also prone to burn out. There is so much going on that new people are immediately drawn into positions of leadership, even heavy-duty positions. Sometimes they are not ready for that. They need a deeper grounding in their faith. Sometimes their feet get ahead of their body.

If people get involved too quickly in activity and the church culture of work, work, work, they do not get a foundation of faith, a deep relationship with Christ, which should be what propels us into action. If you do the action without the foundation, you burn out. You need to be serving out of gratitude and love for God.

A large congregation
where the support staff members do the administrative work.

Marie works as an administrative assistant in the mission department of a very large church. She says:

> The pastors here are very stable, but the support staff turn over constantly. That is because our job feels so meaningless. We are told that our goal is to facilitate lay ministry. We work with congregation members to oversee programs. The members do the visioning and planning and leading, and we do the administrative work.
>
> It is endless and mundane. We fill out room-assignment slips, work-order slips, and rental slips. We route phone calls. The church is growing at a rate of 13 percent a year, but the staff is not, so there is an ever-increasing workload. Sure, we know we are contributing to something significant for the kingdom of God, and that helps, but we are basically administrative cogs in the wheel, doing trivial, unrewarding tasks just to keep things going. And we are supposed to do it all with a smile, so the congregation members feel supported and encouraged in their ministry. I have watched my friends on the church staff burn out and leave. I wonder when it will happen to me.

A congregation
where the same people are approached for money
over and over.

Dov is the rabbi of a large synagogue. He reflects:

> The place I see burnout most clearly in synagogues has to do with fundraising. When there is a significant need, maybe a major building remodel or construction plan, we come to the same people over and over. These are our angels, and it is just not fair to ask them so much. Just because

people are well off does not mean the burden should be solely on them.

It would be better for more people to be involved. It would solidify the community better. In the Jewish community, we do not have the concept of tithing like Christians do, even though it originated with us. So the reality is that we depend over and over on the wealthy.

There is actually an interesting parallel here with volunteerism. Too often, we go to the same people over and over when we need volunteers. We go to the same well too many times. In financial contributing and in volunteering, we need to activate other people in the congregation so they can find points of access and ownership, too.

A small congregation.

Ann has served as interim pastor in several small congregations. She notes:

> In the small church, we encourage burnout because there just are not enough people to do things. The scariest thing in the world in a small church is to say, "Don't worry about what you think you need to do. Just don't do it. If God wants it done, God will raise up someone else to do it." In a small church, you know the life stories of everyone else there, and you know that if you do not do it, the people who will jump in are doing four or six or eight things already, and they should not be doing it any more than you should.
>
> In one church where I served, we adopted a clipboard method of recruitment. People who needed volunteers passed around a clipboard during the announcement time in worship, and people had the opportunity to sign up. We talked about this new method at the board meeting, and the deacons were very nervous about the possibility that some things just might not get enough volunteers, so they might not happen. It is really hard in a small church to let go of things you have been doing. Somehow it plays into our fear that the church might get even smaller and maybe not even survive.

A congregation where people cannot change jobs

Amy attended a Chinese American church for a decade. She remembers:

The Chinese American mentality of slow, steady spirituality, marked by a deep resistance to change, was very evident in that congregation. Serving felt like a prison sentence. There was no honorable discharge. Loyalty and faithfulness were the highest values, and long-term servers were put up as paragons of faithfulness. The Sunday school superintendent had been there for 30 years. The same person had coordinated the coffee hour for 15 years.

I began to find myself wondering, should someone else be trained to do each task? And how can you serve in a fresh way after doing the same thing for so many years?

These six scenarios do not cover, in any systematic way, the kinds of situations in congregations that lead to burnout, but they do give a flavor for the issues involved. We will continue to look at the patterns of congregational life and the personal characteristics that can lead to burnout. But first, we must refine our understanding of what it is.

Defining Burnout

Burning Out versus Rusting Out

I remember seeing a poster sometime in my childhood. It said, "It would be better to burn out than to rust out." That poster shaped my understanding that it's better to give a lot for a high calling than to live a passive, unfocused life. The older I get, however, the more I realize it's still necessary to put some limits around serving and giving.

—Kristin, church staff member

Pastoral counselor John Sanford, in his book *Ministry Burnout*, points out that only recently have we begun to use the word *burnout* to refer to human exhaustion. He wonders if widespread human exhaustion to the level that we call burnout is a relatively new phenomenon. Surely in the past, people became exhausted in a variety of ways. He hypothesizes that this problem has now become so widespread that a special word is needed to describe the condition.

In the past, Sanford notes, the word *burnout* had three meanings not related to people. Burnout can refer to a fire that completely burns the contents of something, usually a building. It can also refer to the breakdown of an electrical circuit caused by high temperatures. Third, burnout is used when a forest fire has been so severe that even the floor of the forest is left bare and deeply damaged, severely slowing the ability of the forest to rebound after the fire.

When we apply these images to human beings, Sanford writes:

We must imagine a man or woman who has been devoured from within by a fiery energy until, like a gutted house, nothing is left. Or we may imagine a person who once carried a current of psychic energy but now, like a burned out electrical conductor, cannot supply power anymore. Or an individual

6

who, like a burned out forest, feels that her power to renew herself has been destroyed. . . . The word "burnout" is drawn from the imagery of fire, and fire is a form and symbol for energy. So in its broadest scope, the problem of burnout is a problem of energy.[3]

Most definitions of burnout do address this issue of energy; most definitions have the word exhaustion or depletion in them. When we are considering congregational volunteers, exhaustion, which manifests itself in lack of interest or enthusiasm for a task, is indeed serious. What helps people maintain their interest in a volunteer position? What helps people continue to bring their whole selves to the task?

The Heart

Susan S. Phillips, a sociologist who teaches the ethics of care at seminaries and who coedited *The Crisis of Care*,[4] has some answers to the questions about why people lose their ability to serve with their whole being.[5] She believes that burnout is caused not by the number of hours a person serves, but by something about how they engage in service. The normal response to a concern about burnout, she says, is to recommend various kinds of disengagement. Don't work so hard, don't do so much, pull back, get more rest. A large body of literature recommends all kinds of coping strategies to avoid burnout, strategies such as lunch with a friend, a vacation, a massage. All of these encourage a balance of engagement and disengagement as the solution to burnout.

The literature on caring, Phillips notes, indicates that the solution does not lie with disengagement. The deeper issue, she believes, is the way we engage with our work or serving. When we engage from the heart, we are more likely to be energized and full in our serving, rather than being drained. This kind of engagement enlarges our capacity for love and promotes growth in us that is rewarding and does not eat us up. This is a moral model rather than an economic model, looking at the concerns of the heart rather than striving for a sophisticated ledger sheet that shows a balance between sources of stress and methods of coping.

The Bible is full of passages that emphasize the heart. Phillips notes:

Hannah prays in her heart, Samuel is said to be a man whose heart is turned towards God, David is the man after God's own heart. The psalms attributed to David frequently mention the heart. We are commanded to return to the Lord with our whole heart and to keep our hearts on right paths. The Bible says our heart melts, trusts, is broken, and is an acceptable sacrifice to God. And in the New Testament, we are told that God searches our hearts.[6]

The recipe for prevention of burnout, Phillips believes, is rediscovering the emphasis on the heart that runs throughout the Bible. The key to healthy serving is an open heart that welcomes God's guidance and correction, a heart that listens to instruction from God. So often, we have a false sense of what the church should be, and we kill ourselves trying to make it happen. These desires originate in a good place with the best intentions, a desire to please God, to build community, to serve others, but we so easily begin to clutch at our own vision. We have our list of things we need to do, and then when we are finished, we can know that we have done them. The mistake is that we have moved into a closed posture that shuts out any awareness of the ongoing presence of God in the tasks to be done, and denies God's ability to guide and shape the tasks as we do them.

Phillips suggests that congregational volunteers consider their place of service and ask themselves what about their serving makes them feel right and energized and full, and what makes them feels like they are doing what they ought to do or makes them feel empty and despairing. As we ask these kinds of questions, we will often find ourselves more aware of old and unresolved issues. She suggests that we need to work to clear out the inner messages from our past that are self-destructive and that keep us functioning in ways that do not engage our hearts.

Our culture so emphasizes the efficiency/management model of control, and congregations fall into that trap so easily. We set a vision, we move forward, we pat ourselves on the back for reaching our goals. It is hard to maintain a heart that is open to God; it is much easier to stay in the saddle with the reins in our own hands. Remaining open to God might involve not meeting a goal. It might involve changing the vision in the middle of a project. It might involve tears. It might be messy.

The Warm Body Mentality

One of the causes of burnout is the warm body mentality—filling a slot with any warm body. It leads to burnout because people aren't doing what they're suited for. It also prevents others from finding their gifts because needs are filled too fast. Sometimes a position needs to be empty for a while so other people can have time to think and pray about whether God is calling them to serve in that way.

—Irene, member of a mid-sized congregation

Grace

The executive of the Seattle Presbytery where I work, Boyd Stockdale, has a slightly different take on burnout.[7] He believes that burnout in congregations originates when people start doing tasks and lose track

8

of why they are doing them. He says, "The moment we forget we are doing things out of spiritual reality, we're toast."

He goes on, "Churches have got to be the most inefficient organizations on God's green earth. There's always more to do. If we start to be there just to keep the church going, we burn out. In reality, the building and the organization are nothing. If we aren't there to build faith, we ought to turn our money over to a more efficient charity."

Our task in congregations is to nurture faith and grow in faith together, and outside of this, nothing matters. A key to nurturing faith, Stockdale believes, is to continually put ourselves in places where we need to rely on God's grace.

He has been shaped by a situation from one of his first pastorates. A woman joined the congregation and threw herself into the life of the church. Her husband and children came now and then, but she was always there, at every church activity. She became indispensable to Stockdale, his right-hand person.

After four years, she came to tell him that she had to quit serving; in fact, she was planning to leave the church. She was going to get a divorce, she said, and because she believed divorce is wrong, she believed she had to leave. He asked her to tell him more about why she felt she had to leave. She said something like this: "I knew that if I could serve so much at church, I would be perfect, and I would earn God's love. Now that I'm going to get a divorce, I won't be perfect any more."

Stockdale was devastated to realize that he had never asked her why she was so involved at church. He reflects, "She felt she could earn God's grace, and none of us knew that. None of us had a conversation with her about her faith for four years. In congregations, we don't understand how destructive our needs for leadership can be. In many ways, it was the church that destroyed that marriage and that family."

He remembers another situation that illustrates a much healthier way to serve. In another one of his congregations, a banker, a formal man and a meticulous dresser, always seemed to be wandering around the children's classrooms looking wistful. When Stockdale asked him why he did not volunteer to work with the children, he said, "I'd love to do that, but I'm a banker and they're always asking me to help with the church finances." Stockdale encouraged him to forget about working with the books and go ahead and volunteer with the kids.

After three years of serving in the church's children's programs, the banker reflected to Stockdale: "Being with the kids challenged all my assumptions about myself. When I first started sitting on the floor

Stopping Some Ministries

We realize that we may have to cease to do things we once had energy for. For example, we used to have a Thanksgiving dinner basket project serving 30 to 40 poor families every year. It was a very labor-intensive project for a week, requiring 25 or more people to participate. One person had made it happen each year, and she came to the place where she could do it no longer. So we said, "This ministry is over." We thanked the woman and prayed for God's guidance to move on. In fact, we made a little bit of a ceremony, celebrating its life and death and our need for God's continual guidance in order to know what to do and not do.

—Mark, pastor of a small congregation

with the kids, I had no idea what to do. I needed to rely on God's grace to help me."

According to Stockdale, churches should be places where people can learn to rely on God's grace in new ways. Sure, it would be more efficient to have a banker tracking the church's finances, but efficiency is not the point. He remembers a time in the 1970s when his denomination mandated a program called "Planning, Budgeting, and Evaluating." The goal was to help congregations manage resources more effectively. Pastors were encouraged to learn from the ways CEOs manage businesses, sessions were supposed to act like boards, and associate pastors were viewed as program developers. The focus shifted to gaining more members and more money. This led to burnout, Stockdale believes, because it encouraged congregations to step out of the real work for which they were called: the study of how to help each other discover God's grace.

A New Neighborhood, A New Environment, A New Century

In the stories I heard about burnout, whether workplace burnout or volunteer burnout, losing heart played a prominent role. In stories about burnout in congregations, I heard a lot about serving out of obligation and duty, which I perceive to be the opposite of grace. So I am convinced of the significance of Susan Phillips's emphasis on heart and Boyd Stockdale's emphasis on grace as we consider the way burnout creeps into congregational life.

Let us look at what is happening at Christ Church to illustrate some of the issues around serving from the heart, motivated by God's grace. Christ Church is typical of many inner-city churches that have been left behind in recent decades as long-time members moved to the suburbs and as their urban neighborhoods changed in ethnic composition.

The people at Christ Church vividly remember their membership coming close to the 2,000 mark four decades ago. Membership and attendance declined gradually throughout the 1970s and 1980s, and attendance leveled out in the early 1990s at about 200. A congregation with 200 people present most Sundays is not a small congregation, but to long-term Christ Church members it feels small, in part because of their history and in part because of their large building. Like many urban churches, Christ Church finds itself in a new neighborhood, a new environment, and a new century without a strong sense of which direction to head.

Maria recently joined the staff of Christ Church as a program director. She reflects:

> This is a congregation with a long history, and that contributes to burnout. There's a weight of history that they carry. They never feel they are living up to the glory days.
>
> The shrinking of the congregation over time contributes to the burnout. In churches, we measure success like the business world—"bigger is better." So as the congregation shrinks, the volume of work for each remaining person increases. In addition, there is constant self-doubt, which really weighs everyone down. "What are we doing wrong that we aren't growing? I don't understand why God is blessing our neighboring churches and not us."
>
> The number of programs is based in a time when there was a larger pool of volunteers. No one is willing to ask, "Realistically, what can we actually do?" So the programs overwhelm the volunteer base and the volunteers are mostly very tired. In addition, creativity is often stifled by the church's long history. "We tried that in 1962, and it didn't work then, so it won't work now." The weight of the history—real or imagined—is at the table in every discussion.

Maria has observed a generational component to burnout at Christ Church. She says, "Sixty percent of the congregation is over 65. They will continue serving no matter how much they hate it. We are attracting more people in their twenties and thirties. They will serve only if they are interested and only as long as they are interested. If programs are poorly run, they are short-term volunteers. And indeed many of the programs here are poorly run, because leaders are overstretched, trying to do too much."

In two particular programs at Christ Church, Maria sees energized volunteers with passion for serving. A rotating women's shelter, housed at the church once a week, and a soup kitchen, which provides food for the many homeless and working poor from the neighborhood, never lack for volunteers.

Maria notes that both of these ministries are intense, yet volunteers do not seem to lose heart. Their contribution is visible and concrete, and their service is live-giving to them. The people in charge of both programs are committed to building community among the volunteers and ministering to them. She observes, "It's the simple things that make

Recognizing Burnout: Questions and Lack of Enthusiasm

I can see burnout in people in meetings. Instead of excitement and forward thinking, I see obvious lack of enthusiasm. I hear questions: "How can we do it? How can I line up all those teachers? How can I get it all done on time?" Also, I can see signs of burnout in body language: shaking of the head, a stressed appearance with tight shoulders. They don't look like they want to be there. They look like they're not enjoying themselves.

—Jennifer, associate pastor at a mid-sized church

the difference. The leaders gather the volunteers for prayer each time they come to serve. They make an effort to listen to what's going on in the volunteers' lives. It's simple really, just people sitting around praying for one another and then going out and helping people in need. In fact, I can see a few other areas at church where passion is developing in areas where people have been very tired. Those are the areas where there has been a lot of intentional prayer."

In her book, *The Overcommitted Christian*, British medical doctor Pamela Evans echoes some of Maria's concerns:

> I need to be willing to ask myself from time to time whether the Lord's service feels like the perfect freedom he intends it to be or whether I've slipped into a spiritual-looking form of bondage, a *hardening of the oughteries*. I need to ask whether my serving is flowing out of my relationship with God or getting in the way of it. The sad thing about putting lots of energy into trying to keep everything going, doing church, showing God how hard we're trying, gritting our teeth and refusing to quit is that it sidetracks us from the intimacy that our heavenly Father wants us to have with him and from the peace he longs to bring to our lives.[8]

One ordained minister used the language of "worshipful work" to describe her goal for her congregational volunteers. She said, "The work of the gospel is going on all the time. God's grace is very active. Our job is to see where the Holy Spirit is at work and get on board. When you do that, you're going to find grace and energy. It really doesn't matter whether or not the task is accomplished. What matters is serving where God is already working. That's what makes our work worshipful."[9] Another pastor told me he believes churches are called to be "communities of joy." His goal is to create a culture where the leaders are blessed in what they do, while working hard and making appropriate sacrifices.

Burnout: A Uniquely Christian Problem?

I interviewed several rabbis for this book, from small and large synagogues, both rural and urban, and all of them reported that burnout among volunteers is not a significant problem in their congregations, except possibly in the area of contributing money. Sure, some people get frustrated with inefficient committees and resign. Sure, some people, particularly older, long-standing members of the synagogue, will serve diligently even when they do not experience a lot of enthusiasm for what they are doing. Sure, the same people get asked to do the same things over and over. But according to these rabbis, burnout among congregational volunteers in synagogues is not common.

Esther, the volunteer coordinator at a medium to large reform synagogue, says that people are forthright when they need to quit serving in a particular position. "I can't do this next year," they say. Esther reflects, "I think of burnout as having a significant visceral component, when you're so exhausted you don't ever want to set foot in that place that got you so tired. We don't see that among volunteers at all. We don't have people leaving because they've gotten too tired. If anything, we see it in our staff." Esther says their challenge is to get new people involved to fill the many volunteer positions that are open. However, burnout among volunteers, she says, seldom happens.

What a contrast with the people I interviewed from Christian congregations. Almost everyone I talked to from Christian congregations—both clergy and lay people—had a burnout story for me, and they told their stories with energy and emotion.

Unitarian Universalist congregations seem to be more like Christian congregations than Jewish congregations in the area of burnout. Because of the long history of volunteerism in U.U. congregations, and because many U.U. congregations started without ordained ministers, members of U.U. congregations and fellowships tend to work hard, with some members overworking significantly. One U.U. minister said to me, "Sacrifice is not a part of our theology, but it's in the culture. It's invisible now, but it still shapes us. People who have been here a long time push themselves to do a lot to keep the congregation functioning."

What makes burnout rare in Jewish congregations? One rabbi told me he thought a key difference between Christian and Jewish congregations was the different perspective on sacrifice. He said, "Sacrifice is not a central theme of the Old Testament stories, and the sacrifices described in the Old Testament are very distant now. We value giving to others based on our concern for justice and our obligation to the community, but there is no encouragement in Judaism to impoverish oneself as we give. We have no call to asceticism."

He went on to talk about the call to balance inherent in Jewish life. Everyone, he said, is called to work, to rest, to spend time with family, and to make some positive difference in the community. All of these responsibilities have equal weight, so there is simply not an emphasis on serving when exhausted or giving until it hurts. There is never any encouragement to neglect family for the sake of another goal.

We will explore the beliefs that lie behind burnout later in this book. We will also discuss the kind of balance that prevents burnout. Someone once said to me that burnout is caused by "oversubscribing to one part of life." The holistic and healthy way of life in the Jewish community encourages people to avoid focusing on only one area of their lives.

A Biblical Burnout Story

Still, things do get out of balance. And God does meet the needs of people who have become depleted. Several Christian writers on burnout cite the story of Elijah in 1 Kings 17–19 as a classic illustration of what burnout looks like and how God ministers to the exhausted person. Elijah's entire ministry involved opposition to King Ahab, married to Queen Jezebel. This renowned queen had imported hundreds of prophets of Baal and Asherah into Samaria, the capital of the northern kingdom, Israel. Elijah foretold a drought that would last several years. He also foretold the end of the drought, which occurred in connection with a great confrontation between himself, a prophet of Yahweh, and the hundreds of prophets of Baal and Asherah.

The confrontation was decisive, and the victory for Yahweh was clear—and it left Elijah exhausted. Jezebel promised to kill him, and he fled—to save his life, to escape exhaustion and fear, to find solace and comfort after a miracle and a battle. We can easily imagine the swirl of emotions that must have accompanied Elijah as he ran.

After a day's journey, he sat down under a solitary tree and asked to die. "It is enough; now, O Lord, take away my life, for I am no better than my ancestors" (1 Kings 19:4). "It is enough," or, as another translation puts it, "I have had enough," is a classic expression of burnout.

God's response is immediate. An angel comes and feeds Elijah twice. Then Elijah walks south to Mount Horeb, a journey that takes 40 days and 40 nights. After he arrives, God asks him what he is doing there and he responds: "I have been very zealous for the Lord, the God of hosts; for the Israelites have forsaken your covenant, thrown down your altars, and killed your prophets with the sword. I alone am left, and they are seeking my life, to take it away" (1 Kings 19:10).

God answers him in two ways. First, God "passes by" and shows Elijah his presence in a "sound of sheer silence." Then God gives Elijah specific instructions of what he is to do next, which includes the anointing of Elisha as his successor (1 Kings 19:11-18).

I find it remarkable that God does not criticize Elijah in any way for coming to the place where all he can say is, "I have had enough."

Instead, God immediately meets his needs in a variety of ways. In *Beating Burnout*, physician Frank Minirth and his coauthors discuss God's compassionate response to Elijah's need:

> First, He met Elijah's physical needs—rest and nourishment (vv. 5-6). Second, God allowed Elijah to see that He still remained in control of circumstances and was still active in the prophet's life. The extended communication between the two of them (vv. 9-17) demonstrates God's continued concern for the prophet. Third, during that communication, God prompted Elijah to ventilate his intense feelings. To get rid of negative feelings, it is important not to bury them but to express them. . . . Fourth, only after Elijah had exposed his feelings did God give him new but lighter tasks. . . . And finally, God provided for Elijah something every burnout victim needs after his recovery: a genuine friend. From that point on, Elisha became Elijah's friend, fellow worker and disciple.[10]

British physician Pamela Evans notes that Elijah's saying "I have had enough" was a starting point of healing and restoration. She believes it is significant that the process began with physical refreshment. She writes, "So often when we or others are burned out, we feel the need to do something religious. That's not how God dealt with Elijah. I don't believe God is nearly as religious as we make him out to be."[11]

Evans writes that she often suggests to weary or frustrated Christians that they go down to the beach and throw stones in the sea. She believes that this apparently pointless activity helps people experience the reality that God can call us to activities that have no other purpose than refreshment. She cites Matt. 11:29 in *The Message*, where Jesus says, "Get away with me and you'll recover your life. I'll show you how to take a real rest." [12]

God Will Provide Healing

I believe God calls congregational leaders to do everything they can to make burnout a rare event in their congregations. But when burnout does occur, congregational leaders can come alongside their members with confidence and anticipation that God will be about the business of bringing healing and enabling restoration. That healing will probably involve physical rest and renewal, as it did in Elijah's case. It will involve expression of all the maelstrom of negative feelings; congregational leaders will probably hear more than they want to about the pain and frustration that has come from intense service. In the midst of listening, they can encourage the burned-out person to bring those feelings to God as well.

In time, God's healing for burnout will involve a renewed call to service and a renewed involvement in community. In time, healing will result in renewed energy, renewed desire to risk whatever it takes to experience God's grace, and a renewed ability to serve from the heart. We can pray and watch for these signs of health as we come alongside people in pain.

2
WORKPLACE BURNOUT AND IMPLICATIONS FOR CONGREGATIONS

The most stressful workplaces are those where a demanding pace is coupled with virtually no individual discretion.

—Juliet Schorr[1]

Burnout in the workplace is significantly different in some ways from burnout among congregational volunteers. To understand congregational burnout, however, we need to begin by developing a basic understanding of workplace burnout for several reasons. First, burnout was initially identified in the workplace, and almost all the research on burnout has been conducted in workplaces, so we need to start there to understand many of the issues

Second, the people in our congregations do not lead compartmentalized lives. Burnout in one arena will affect the other parts of our lives. Some will bring their exhaustion from workplace burnout to their congregation, hoping for some spiritual insight that will lead to health and healing. Some will be on the edge of burnout both at work and in their volunteer positions. Some will treat their volunteer positions in the congregation almost like a job, and if they burn out there, the burnout will resemble workplace burnout.

Third, many congregations depend on support staff to do much of the ministry, and in some congregations they burn out at an alarming rate. Their burnout is definitely workplace burnout but will often have an additional overlay of the guilt, feelings of failure, and disappointment with God that are seen in congregational burnout.

And fourth, although workplace burnout differs in some significant ways from burnout in a congregation, a surprising number of aspects are similar, even virtually identical. As we study workplace burnout, we will notice the many parallels with burnout in a congregation.

We will begin by looking at three stories of workplace burnout that illustrate many of the issues. We will also look at some of the research about workplace burnout, and make connections with what happens in congregations.

Sylvia's Story

Sister Sylvia is a Roman Catholic nun in her late fifties. A little less than 20 years ago, she experienced a very significant episode of burnout, significant both for its intensity and also for the impact on her later life. Her story is a good place to begin to look at workplace burnout, because some of the theological issues that we see in congregational burnout are also present.

Before talking about her situation, Sylvia reflected on what it's like to be a Roman Catholic nun.

Any Catholic sister brings an added dimension to life because we view our lives as totally dedicated to prayer and apostolic service. The vocation can set you up for overwork. The dedication, the "shoulds," the "oughts." We're meant to be servants like Jesus. When a difficult task comes up, there is never a question that you can't do it all. The religious life takes your energy but sets you up to believe you can do anything "by God's grace." We believe God can give you the grace to do anything, even teach violin even if you've never played it.

When Sylvia was 33, she was asked to be the principal of a large Catholic high school. The job was very demanding because of the high standards she set for herself. She believed she needed to be at every school event, from girl's soccer to football games to chess club. She tried to look over every student's schedule and go to national education meetings. At the same time, she was finishing her master's degree and working on a doctorate, nurturing a counseling ministry on the side, and speaking at churches.

After nearly 10 years on the job, she found she couldn't sleep. She could see clearly that she was having some kind of an anxiety reaction. She experienced lack of concentration, fears about her health, coupled with a strong desire to keep going. She says:

Finally, I was hospitalized for 10 weeks in two different hospitals. While I was in the first hospital, I was administering the Myers-Briggs Type Indicator to the nurses! I just couldn't stop. Finally, in the second hospital, a combination of

18

medication and therapy enabled me to step back and look at my life, what I was doing to myself and what I was doing to my giftedness.

There was a garden in a park near that second hospital, and one day I noticed a red flower on a cactus. I realized I had missed half of life because I hadn't noticed the beauty around me. I cried because I had missed so much. Later the same thing happened when I saw a winter cardinal in a garden.

What is the message of the winter cardinal? It called me to claim my life back from burnout, to slow down. I began to see the importance of relationships, not roles. I saw more clearly the enticement to believe that I can do everything. I also saw that it's not selfish to look after our own needs, even when we're called to ministry.

After the hospitalization, it took Sylvia another year and a half to completely recover. First she worked in a parish. She loved the work, but could see herself starting down the burnout road. Then she was assigned to work in the office of a bishop, who turned out to be a wonderful model for her. "He was a man of prayer and great love for people. He also had a strong sense of who he was, what he could do and what he couldn't do. He wasn't fearful of saying, 'I can't do that.' He didn't seem to feel the need to live up to expectations from outside. He was truly at home with who he was."

In her job in the bishop's office, Sylvia again got involved in ten things, but there was some difference. She kept remembering the call of the winter cardinal, and she tried to learn from the model of the bishop. She also developed supportive relationships. "It was still dangerous," she says. "I kept getting close to that major trap where we base our value on what we do. We become too intense, we think we have to solve all problems, we give too little time to relationships that could nurture us."

Now Sylvia has only two major aspects to her job, instead of ten. It was very hard for her to cut back to two things. She needed the support of her friends saying, "cutting back doesn't mean you're not competent or young any more." She says,

My saving grace was friends who loved me enough to say that it's not how much you do that defines you, it's how much you're at home with yourself.

I find the people I most admire are those who are at home with themselves. When they meet you, they greet you

Recognizing Burnout: Stress-Related High Blood Pressure

I was chairing the deacon board when we had a significant conflict. One of the deacons wanted to move in a direction different from the rest of us, and he organized a faction of church around his vision. The conflict went on for months. I could see the burnout beginning among the deacons when a couple of them went to the doctor with elevated blood pressure. The doctor said it was stress-related. People would say they were having trouble sleeping. I began to find myself thinking, "I've had it. Let's leave and start our own house church." I had been teaching adult Sunday school for years. As the conflict wore on month after month, I would wake up on Sunday mornings feeling physically sick because I didn't want to be there.

—Rod, member of a small congregation

as if you're the only person in their life. They're not distracted by the tasks on their desk. They know they can't accomplish everything. How do we pray if we don't have the ability to be at home with ourselves and give time to that which is the inner compass of our lives? Burnout for me was being given a second chance to find home, a second chance to decide what to live for.

Jim's Story

As Jim looks back, he can see that he was suffering from burnout for many years before retirement. But he persevered and actually did some of his best work during those last years of work. His lectures got rave reviews. When he published an article, the feedback was enthusiastic. He was indispensable in his role as dean of the doctor of education program he had founded more than a decade earlier. An endless stream of small crises required his expertise and experience and proved his value. The program was turning out knowledgeable and strategic-thinking graduates who he believed might change the face of education.

But for many years before retirement, Jim could barely get up in the morning. The weight of boredom, exhaustion, and routine pressed on him from all sides. The lassitude spilled over into all his activities. Even the gardening and tennis he had enjoyed all his adult life seemed boring and futile. He was curt and impatient with the other faculty members, he was short and irritable with his wife, and when his grown children stopped by, he could barely bring himself to talk to them.

Throughout Jim's career, he had never stayed in one job or position more than six years. He had known intuitively that he needed frequent change. But things were different when he achieved his dream, the creation of a progressive, cutting-edge doctor of education degree program at a major university. He knew he needed to move on, but he just could not let go of his baby, his dream. Every time someone came along who could have assumed some of the administrative responsibility, a small or large crisis arose that made Jim feel indispensable. So he stayed on and became more and more exhausted.

He stayed on until retirement, a total of 15 years in the same position. Now, a decade later, he looks back from a position of restored energy and enthusiasm for life. He knows he made a serious mistake by staying as dean too long, but at the time he could not seem to do anything different.

Max's Story

The setting for Max's burnout story is also a major university, but his personality and the issues around his experience are very different from Jim's. Max, a pediatrician, was invited to join the faculty of a medical school when he was 30. He felt a strong call to full-time teaching. He remembered his own frustrations in medical school, and he felt a real challenge and joy in creating courses that would help medical students learn in a supportive environment. For each of his classes he designed a detailed workbook to explain complex procedures step-by-step. Students loved his classes because he so obviously cared for the students and their needs and concerns.

Max never felt much sense of comradeship with the other faculty, but the good relationships with the students made up for that lack. After teaching for several years, his position became a tenure-track position, and he realized he needed to publish many more articles to get tenure. He put his teaching on autopilot and dived into research, which he did not enjoy nearly as much as teaching, but he knew it was necessary in order to continue to teach.

In the middle of his quest for tenure, a new department chair came from Australia to head the department. He completely changed the way the courses were taught, using an Australian education model. Now, instead of each faculty person being solely in charge of a certain number of courses, each course was taught by a large team of professors. Max found that he was assigned a few lectures in a large number of courses. No longer could he get to know the students in the same way, and no longer could he use his detailed workbooks. He felt his teaching was much less effective, but in the drive to do research to get tenure, he did not really take time to worry about it.

He got tenure. He was immediately eligible for a sabbatical, and he took a year to study medical ethics, one of his interests. He had pioneered the ethics course at the medical school a few years earlier and he felt he needed more background knowledge. When he came back to teaching after the sabbatical, he found his colleagues less supportive than ever. They were unable to see how the study of ethics related to pediatrics. They thought he was wasting his time.

In addition, he no longer had close relationships with students because of the way the courses were structured with a large team of faculty for each class. He found himself on several boring committees. He realized his department chair had been sparing him from onerous committee assignments while he was working for tenure. His paycheck was also a source of frustration. In the years immediately after he got tenure, the state legislature provided funds for very skimpy faculty raises, so there was little positive financial reward.

There was no joy in his work, and he started dreading weekdays. His sleep was badly interrupted. He experienced increased stomachaches. He was irritable and negative. His doctor put him on an anti-depressant.

He lasted four years after returning from his sabbatical. Because of his strong sense of call to teaching, Max found it wrenching to leave the university, but he knew he had to do it for his own health. He went into medical practice. In his first decade away from the university, he worked in several different clinics before he found what he wanted: a place with congenial relationships. One thing he learned from his burnout experience was the importance to him of harmonious relationships at work.

Max never again experienced a sense of call to his work. He is able to work part-time as a pediatrician and engage in a variety of volunteer activities. He feels a greater sense of call to his volunteering than he does to his work. He misses that sense of certainty and purpose he had in his early years of teaching.

Reflecting on the Stories

In the three stories we can see several patterns that are relevant to burnout in congregations. Both Sister Sylvia and Jim burned out because of forces at work within them. Sylvia held herself to incredibly high standards in the school where she was principal, and she pushed herself to take on speaking and counseling engagements, in addition to working on graduate degrees. She was driven to do far too much. Jim knew on some level that he needed to leave his position as dean, but he just could not let go.

Max's burnout came more from forces outside himself. The lack of control, lack of rewards, and lack of congenial relationships he experienced at work are classic signs of a workplace that fosters burnout. Burnout can be caused by forces within a person or by the environment where they work, or a combination of both. This is true of both the workplace and places where people volunteer.

Jim's story illustrates another significant point. We tend to think that people who are burning out will appear tired and lackluster in their performance. During Jim's years of burnout, he was doing his best work. If anything, his competence increased as he burned out. Sylvia showed some of this too, as she continued to try to care for people while she was in the hospital. This is not uncommon in the workplace. In congregations, we may also find high-functioning people who are actually in the middle of burnout.

For both Sylvia and Max, significant theological issues lay behind their burnout. Sylvia had been taught as a Catholic nun that anything is possible with God's grace; she took that to mean that God's grace would enable her to work endless hours without respite. She had to learn that God's grace also involves balance and rest. Max had felt a strong sense of call from God to teaching. His sense of call made it hard for him to acknowledge the ways teaching just wasn't right any more.

Theological beliefs often lie behind burnout at church. A sense of call might prevent someone from leaving a place of service even if that place has changed so much that remaining becomes destructive. A belief such as, "I can do all things through him who strengthens me" (Phil. 4:13), might motivate someone to serve in ways that are so far beyond their capacity that burnout is inevitable. As we move through this book, we will see other theological issues that lie behind burnout.

The Symptoms of Burnout

We saw in the three stories some of the various physical symptoms and emotional responses to burnout. Both Jim and Max had a hard time getting up in the morning and going to work when they were burning out. Both reported being irritable. Max and Sylvia talked about patterns of sleeplessness. Max had stomachaches. Sylvia had a lot of anxiety. I am mentioning physical symptoms here because sometimes these symptoms are interpreted as purely physical and medical problems, quite apart from the stress in our lives. We need to pay attention to physical symptoms because they might indicate approaching burnout.

Researcher Elizabeth Layman writes, "Victims of emotional burnout exhibit physical and behavioral signs. Physically, burned out people have headaches and gastrointestinal complaints. Behaviorally, they are easily angered, overly confident, and chronically cynical. They may become workaholics. Psychologically, burned out people lose their enthusiasm and motivation."[2]

Over the course of two years, I led several daylong seminars on workplace burnout. In the seminars, I asked participants to list the physical complaints they associated with burnout. The lists were long:

- insomnia
- heart problems

- allergies
- stomach problems
- headaches
- arthritis
- skin problems
- recurrent flu, colds, and sore throats
- menstrual problems
- muscle aches and stiffness
- lack of sexual desire
- eating problems, including weight loss or weight gain
- addictions
- problems with the back or neck
- high blood pressure

Burnout Caused by Feeling Powerless

My friend, Ellie, agreed to serve as worship elder in our congregation because she believed that her significant leadership experience would help her make a difference. She is principal of a large urban high school and holds a Ph.D. in education. She joined the elder board just as the pastor and choir director began to initiate a discussion about reducing the size of the elder board and eliminating the worship elder position. Over and over she spoke up in meetings about the significance of having lay people involved as a part of the decision-making process about worship. In the discussions she felt

(continued)

All of these physical complaints can turn up among volunteers who are burning out, although most of them are not very common. Sleeplessness, however, stands out as a common physical symptom of burnout both in the workplace and in congregations.

When we make a list of emotional and psychological characteristics of workplace burnout in seminars, participants mention the characteristics of exhaustion and depletion that we would expect, along with irritability, cynicism, discouragement, negative attitudes towards work and people, and "clamming up." Burnout and depression can appear at the same time, which is visible in Max's story.

Participants also mentioned Internet and Nintendo obsession as symptoms of burnout, along with numbness, inability to rest, and a feeling of isolation. Perhaps most poignant was one person who said in burnout that she "lost her inner compass"; she lost a sense that she was functioning normally and she felt she was not herself.

An unexpected symptom of burnout can be an increased desire for control and a need to keep producing even when exhausted. Lots of people experience overconfidence when they burn out, and tend to overfunction, striving even harder to stay in control and exercise competence. We saw glimpses of this in both Sylvia and Jim. People who are burning out sometimes view themselves as more indispensable than ever before, and they are less willing to relinquish responsibilities to others. This is common among volunteers and staff in congregations as well as the workplace.

Researchers emphasize that burnout is a process rather than a discrete event. According to one researcher, it is the "final step in a progression of unsuccessful attempts to cope with a variety of negative stress conditions."[3] Most of the people I interviewed about their burnout experience talked about the way they could recognize it clearly after it happened. At the time, it seemed to creep up on them in almost imperceptible stages. Even though they experienced some of the symptoms described above, they were not able to identify those symptoms as warnings that burnout was approaching. They were simply not aware of the cumulative effect of stress in their bodies, souls, and spirits.

Stress and Coping Strategies

As Susan Phillips mentioned in the first chapter, most of the research on burnout focuses on the balance of stress and coping strategies. It is easy to think that the people under the most stress would be the most obvious candidates for burnout, but the research shows that some of the people who experience a great deal of stress also have effective coping strategies that alleviate the stress and enable them to work at a fast and intense pace year after year.

One person I interviewed told me, "I can work ten-hour days six days a week indefinitely, as long as I have one day each week off and one month each year of real vacation." He is nearing the end of a long career in a stressful position in his denomination, and his energy, enthusiasm, and light heart are visible to anyone who talks to him. In my interview with him, he had a good time telling me all the athletic activities he enjoys on his day off and on his vacation. He understands clearly what coping strategies work for him.

Coping strategies can be physical, social, cognitive, psychological, or spiritual. Some people, like the man I just mentioned who loves physical exercise, have one major coping mechanism. Other people have lots of different ways to relax and let go of stress, such as lunches with friends, long bubble baths, reading quietly with scented candles burning, and gardening. They have learned how to unwind and keep the stress from debilitating them.

Still, the stressors build up. And in many different jobs, the workplace has never been as stressful as it is now. If you asked Max, the pediatrician who burned out teaching at the university, if he had tried various coping strategies to help him with the stress of his work, he would say yes, emphatically. He exercised, took regular days off, went on interesting and satisfying vacations, enjoyed dates with his wife, and played tennis with his kids. But the coping strategies simply could not balance the stress. Somehow, he lost heart, and all the coping strategies in the world could not make up for that.

condescended to and her words seemed to have no influence. After a year, the frustration of feeling powerless accumulated to the point where she resigned from the board and vowed never to take another leadership position in our congregation.

—Kelly, member of a large congregation

In her vivid book *Toxic Work*, Barbara Bailey Reinhold discusses the many ways our assumptions about work have been turned upside down in recent years.[4] In the past, people assumed that employers would be concerned about the well-being of their employees and give them a reasonable workload. Now the short-term mentality in most workplaces has convinced many people that employees are viewed by employers as one more disposable asset.

Reinhold talks about the many different stressors that are more common in the workplace than ever before. She describes six symptoms of stress she sees frequently today:

1. anxiety: when you can't stop thinking about it
2. anger: when you're mad more than you want to be
3. lack of control: when your life is running away with you
4. lack of confidence: when you're not sure you can do it
5. shut-down feelings: when you don't feel much anymore
6. diminished relationships: when there's not much joy in connecting[5]

Reinhold stresses the importance of listening to our bodies. Our bodies will respond to stress and manifest the kinds of symptoms listed a few pages ago. They will let us know that something is not right. Reinhold believes that career stress is the greatest health problem for working adults. She notes that many studies show that work satisfaction increases both health and longevity.

Christina Maslach, one of the earliest researchers on burnout, agrees that the workplace can be more stressful than ever before. She has isolated six characteristics of a workplace that elevates stress levels to the point where burnout is very possible:

1. We feel overloaded.
2. We feel lack of control over what we do.
3. We are not rewarded for what we do.
4. We are experiencing a breakdown in community.
5. We are not treated fairly.
6. We're dealing with conflicting values.

In Max's story at the beginning of the chapter, we can see five of these stressors. He felt overloaded with boring committee assignments, he no longer had control of structuring and teaching his own courses, he did not receive significant salary raises (rewards), he did not experience a sense of community with the other faculty, and his interest in ethics was ignored by his colleagues because their values were different from his. According to Maslach, it is totally reasonable that he would have experienced burnout. It would be very difficult to develop and nurture coping strategies that would enable Max to deal effectively with such a high degree of mismatch and stress in a job setting. It is very hard to continue to serve from the heart in the kind of workplace Maslach describes.

Maslach also lists six corresponding characteristics of a workplace where burnout is unlikely:

1. sustainable workload
2. feelings of choice and control
3. recognition and reward
4. a sense of community
5. fairness, respect, and justice
6. meaningful and valued work[6]

If we want to help congregation members who are struggling with burnout at work, we can use these lists to help them evaluate the cumulative stress of their workplace. These lists can help with making the decision to stay with or leave a particular job.

These lists can also be used to get feedback from support staff in congregations. Is their workload manageable? Are they feeling they have choices and control? Do they have a sense of community? Do they feel their work is meaningful and valued?

In addition, these lists are very helpful in evaluating congregational service opportunities. Each of the six characteristics of a healthy workplace can just as effectively describe healthy places to serve in congregations. Many of the congregational burnout stories I heard involved the issues described in these lists.

Balance

As I have studied and taught about burnout issues in the past few years, I tried to come up with my own definitions of burnout. One definition I tried out for a while goes like this: *Burnout is exhaustion caused by a chronic stress overload coupled with too few effective coping strategies.* This definition draws on the burnout research focusing on stress and coping strategies. I like to use the word *chronic* in the definition because it emphasizes the ongoing nature of the stressors that lead to burnout. As we said earlier, burnout is not a discrete event; instead, it is a process of gradually increasing exhaustion.

Recognizing Burnout: We Don't Know How to Find the Energy to Do What Needs to Be Done

I watched two new churches dissolve after several years of trying to make a go of it. They were very different congregations, one liberal and one conservative, but at the end the leaders were using almost the exact same language to describe the burnout they felt. People in both congregations said things like this: "We really like each other, but we're really worn out. We've worked on this so long, we feel it's our duty to continue, but we don't know how to find the energy to do what needs to be done." And, "I just can't keep this up; I don't even want to come anymore."

—Tom, a presbytery executive

Here is another definition I worked with for a while: *Burnout is progressive depletion caused by a chronic lack of balance.* This definition emphasizes that we all need balance in our lives. We need coping strategies that balance the stressors. We need time with family and accepting friends to balance the challenge of working with demanding people. We need quiet time alone as well as time with people. We need physical exercise, especially if we have sedentary jobs.

We need a certain kind of balance within our work as well. Some people believe that burnout is caused by overuse of strengths; others believe burnout is caused by overuse of our weak areas. It is hard to judge in another person's life, but it appears that in the cases of Sylvia and Jim, at the beginning of the chapter, they overused their strengths and kept on functioning out of their strong areas long after they should have stopped. In Max's case, it appears that as the years went by in teaching, he had less and less opportunity to use his strengths, and thus he was continually working out of his weak areas all the time.

Research seems to indicate that the people who do not burn out possess a balance in their work life between using their strengths and growing in developing their weak areas. Part of being a healthy human being is to grow and develop and embrace new challenges. Yet we were created to use our gifts and abilities. A healthy work environment will give us opportunity for both.

And we do need play time as well as work time. Psychologist Judith Provost points out that there are two kinds of play: compensatory and spillover.[7] In compensatory play, we are balancing other things in our lives. The social worker who does intricate woodworking, the secretary who works out intensely, and the banker who takes up ballroom dancing are all engaging in recreational activities that provide balance to their work life. They are compensating in their play for what is missing in their work.

My father-in-law, who adored his work and never experienced a moment of burnout, engaged in what Provost calls spillover play. He worked as an engineer designing bookmobiles and vehicles for blood banks, and at home he worked in his workshop designing such things as mailboxes that would swing aside when hit by cars. His work spilled over into his play, and for him, there was no problem in this pattern.

Provost lists the needs satisfied through play: psychological, educational, social, relaxational, physiological, and aesthetic.[8] Her list can be helpful in evaluating the ways that recreational activities can provide balance to work, and it can help us discern the kinds of play that might be most rejuvenating for us.

Provost's use of the word *play* instead of *recreation* or *weekend activities* can raise cautions for people who believe that all of life should be seriously devoted to work and service. And that brings us to the issue of the beliefs that lie behind burnout.

I have listed all these aspects of balance because I do believe lack of balance contributes to both workplace and congregational burnout. In chapter 1 we saw the significance of serving from the heart, motivated by grace. I also wanted you to see the issues of balance that play into burnout. In addition, our beliefs—often unstated—play a part.

Beliefs that Foster Burnout

In my seminars on burnout, participants became animated when I asked them to tell me the beliefs that lie behind burnout. In fact, I had a hard time moving them on to another topic. As they called out various sayings they had lived by or watched other people live by, there was a rueful sense of amazement at how easy it is to fall into various kinds of damaging or warped beliefs. Here is a list of some of the beliefs that foster an attitude that we should continue to work beyond fatigue and beyond a sensible stopping point:

- If I don't do it, it won't get done.
- No one can do it as well as I can.
- There will be plenty of time for rest and fun later on.
- If I say no, there will be negative consequences for me.
- I'm personally responsible to see that this gets done.
- I can't be pleased with myself unless I'm exhausted.
- I don't have a right to be here unless I'm exhausted.
- I can't give up.
- I can't make major changes now; I've just got to keep going.
- I have to be perfect: loving, serving, giving, caring, having an orderly house, having perfect children, changing the world.

It makes me feel tired just to read those statements. As I read them, however, I realize how easily I am sucked into believing them. And some of the statements have aspects of truth to them. It may be true that if I say no, I will experience negative consequences. It also may be true that if I don't do it, it won't get done. But those statements might also prove not be true. And if I want to embrace health, I need to delete those statements from my core beliefs, even if there are kernels of truth in some of them.

Some of these statements come from damaging things we learned as children and from our inadequate sense of God's grace. Most people of faith would not want to assert that we only have worth if we are exhausted. Most would not want people to believe that they have to be perfect. Yet those beliefs can be deep-seated and hard to change.

In religious settings, some of our core beliefs center around the need to sacrifice and obey God's call to serve the world. Those beliefs are based in truth, but they need to be balanced by an additional set of truths around God's provision for the world, our limits as finite creatures, God's call to rest, and God's desire that we live in grace. All too often, our beliefs about service, sacrifice, and hard work stand on their own without the balancing beliefs about grace and rest.

Healing from Burnout

We have seen in Sister Sylvia's story that for her, healing involved reframing some of her beliefs about the importance of continual service, the value of rest, and the fact that our identity comes from being loved by God, not from what we do. For her, healing came through medication that slowed her down, therapy, time in reflection, and the counsel of good friends.

A social worker who burned out from an increasingly challenging case load and the overwhelming burden of more and more paperwork says it took her a year and a half to be healed. As a very conscientious and responsible worker, she stayed on at work long enough to train her successor. Then she took the entire summer off. She cleaned closets, spent a lot of time alone, and tried to engage in lots of sensory activities to balance the heavily relational and conceptual aspects of the job where she burned out.

In the fall she returned to school to get an advanced degree, and she found that studying continued her healing process. She has now moved into a different profession. Reflecting on her burnout, she says, "I'm less ambitious now, more assertive, more able to say no. I have more boundaries now around what I will take on and what I will say no to. I'm a much wiser person now."

In *Beating Burnout*, Frank Minirth and his coauthors tell the story of a woman who burned out because of the high standards she kept for herself. Describing her healing, this woman said, "I first recognized that I was burned out; then I began to do something about it. I learned to take care of myself physically. I cultivated my spiritual life. I developed outside interests. And perhaps most important of all, I learned not to be so hard on myself, to allow myself to fail occasionally, and to forgive myself when I did fail."[9]

Another person who had worked in a technical and supervisory position in a computer chip factory said that for her, healing from burnout involved moving into a totally different position, this time in human resources. She took two months off work before changing positions, and when she took the human resources job, she was very aware that the new position was much more aligned with her personal mission statement. She says the burnout experience taught her how to rest and take better care of herself.

Healing takes time. Whether it is workplace burnout or burnout in a volunteer position, people talk about the healing process lasting for months, a year, sometimes 18 months or two years. With workplace burnout, the long healing is necessary because of the depth of exhaustion. With burnout in a congregation, the faith issues that are triggered by burnout often take a long time to resolve, and there may be significant physical and emotional exhaustion as well. Healing is simply not a fast process.

Implications for Congregations

I have written at length about workplace burnout. Congregational leaders need to know about it because we are serving congregations where many members are vulnerable to workplace burnout, either because the workplaces themselves are toxic or because the people carry inner beliefs and habits that drive them towards burnout. We need to be conscious of the stresses faced in the workplace by our members, and we need to try to create a worshipful and healing environment in our congregations where members can find rest and healing for the forces that drive them towards burnout in all areas of life. A rabbi told me he has noticed that people who tend towards workaholism often look to religion to help them find their way back to their families and to a deeper attachment to significant values.

As we consider workplace burnout, we can see similarities with burnout among volunteers in congregations. People stay in jobs too long, growing depleted and exhausted because of their values, beliefs, and sense of calling. In the same way, people in congregations sometimes stay in volunteer positions too long because of their values, beliefs, and sense of calling.

People who are burning out have a variety of physical and emotional symptoms, and many of the same symptoms occur in workplace burnout and congregational burnout. I heard stories about sleeplessness and discouragement, numbness and feelings of isolation from people suffering from burnout in both the workplace and in congregations. Stressors in both the workplace and in congregations

Being Honest about Where I Fit into Others' Ideas

I knew I was close to burnout in my volunteer position at church because I was experiencing frustration, tension, and depression. I could feel a lack of interest in continuing. Since that near-burnout experience, I've learned that not everything is going to work. Other people aren't as dedicated to your idea as you are. They don't see the need to make an extra effort. Now I try to be responsible when I'm on the receiving end of other people's ideas. I try to let them know where I fit, or don't fit, into their ideas.

—Carol, member of a small congregation

can cause the same kinds of responses: anxiety, anger, lack of control, lack of confidence, shut-down feelings, and diminished relationships.

Christina Maslach's list of characteristics of workplaces that foster burnout and those that foster health is directly applicable to congregations. Earlier I mentioned using her list with church staff. In addition, the leaders of any congregational ministry can take Maslach's list describing a healthy workplace and use it to evaluate the way they run their ministry. They can ask these questions of volunteers, drawn directly from Maslach's lists: Is the workload sustainable? Do the volunteers have feelings of choice and control? Are there appropriate and loving expressions of recognition and reward? Do the activities of the ministry foster a sense of community? Do the participants experience a sense of fairness, respect, and justice? Does their serving feel meaningful to them?

Issues of balance are relevant in both workplace and congregational burnout. As I mentioned in the first chapter, someone once said to me that burnout is caused by "oversubscribing to one part of life." You can see people who put so much weight on their jobs that they have become disconnected from their family. In the same way, congregational volunteers seem to easily oversubscribe to one aspect of congregational life: constantly serving in the kitchen without participating in prayer and spiritual nurture, constantly teaching the children without attending classes for adults where they could learn and grow, or always bustling about during worship services—ushering or performing music without slowing down to participate in worship themselves.

Another parallel between workplace burnout and congregational burnout is the time required for healing. A woman I know talked to me about her friend, who had served way too long leading a music group in his congregation. She said, "I told him it will take months, maybe even a year, before he feels like doing anything at church. That's burnout for you. People think they will heal in a few weeks, but there's something about that deep exhaustion that just takes a lot of time. I told him to be patient with himself, and the desire to serve and be involved will come back. In time."

My Favorite Definition

As we wrap up these two introductory chapters about burnout, you may wonder which definition of burnout I have settled on. A good definition, I believe, would certainly express the deep exhaustion or depletion that lies at the heart of burnout. Other central issues include losing heart, no longer experiencing joy in the very activities that used to be life giving, and chronic lack of balance or oversubscription to one part of life. Too much stress over the long term, coupled with too few coping strategies, could also be mentioned. Deep-seated beliefs that influence behavior are also significant.

In the seminars I taught on burnout, I usually invited the participants to work together as a group to come up with a definition of burnout. In one particular seminar, the participants wanted to create a definition that covered all the symptoms and as many of the main issues as possible. They came up with a very long definition! That is my temptation as well.

In the end, however, I have settled on a favorite definition that mentions none of the central issues I have named, but somehow captures the essence of burnout. This definition comes from a newspaper interview with business consultant Robin Sheerer, author of an excellent book on workplace burnout, *No More Blue Mondays*. Burnout, Sheerer says, is when "the body's doing the work, but the spirit's not present."[10]

3

WHAT CONGREGATIONS CAN DO
IDENTIFYING AND PREVENTING BURNOUT

It's all too easy to work the treadmill called church *until we're worn out and alienated from our families.*
—Pamela Evans, *The Overcommitted Christian*[1]

During the time I was writing and researching this book, I was amazed at how many people wanted to tell me a personal burnout story when I mentioned that I was writing a book about burnout in congregations. I was also amazed at the intensity of emotion in most of the people who told me stories. "Burnout in faith communities is wrong!" they seemed to be saying. "It shouldn't happen in churches and synagogues, which are dedicated to promoting spiritual health! Congregational leaders should do something about it and make sure it stops happening!"

It is a tall order and an impossible mission to eliminate all burnout in congregations. But we can reduce burnout by paying attention to the attitudes and structures that make it more likely to happen. In this chapter, we will look at some of the patterns of burnout in congregations, and then we will consider some of the congregational practices that make burnout less likely. We will begin with several stories.

Eric and Kim's Story

Eric and Kim attended Calvin Presbyterian Church, a midsized congregation, while they were graduate students at a nearby university. Both were in their mid-twenties when they finished their degrees. They got jobs and decided to get more involved at church. As undergraduates and graduate students, they had been very involved in a campus Christian ministry, leading Bible studies and other events, so they knew they would be able to help in some significant way at Calvin.

Recognizing Burnout: Symptoms to Watch For

Here are some of the symptoms that let me know a volunteer is close to burnout:

- frustration and irritation over small things
- lack of creativity
- lack of enthusiasm and energy
- complaining or withdrawing
- arriving late
- not doing the job as well, or barely doing it at all
- using these words often: "I am really tired of . . ."

All of these can be symptoms of other things, but when I see these symptoms, I watch for burnout.

—Elizabeth, director of children's ministries in a large congregation

Mary, who served on Calvin's staff as director of adult ministries, recognized Eric's and Kim's maturity and gifts for ministry, and she approached them with an idea. Calvin's singles group had been floundering for several years, and it seemed to be on its last legs. Mary proposed that Eric and Kim try to start a fellowship group for people in their twenties, married and single.

Eric and Kim agreed to pray about it. As they prayed, they came to the conclusion that this was just what they were looking for. They had been married two years by now, so their marriage was solidly established. Both of them enjoyed the kind of challenge this ministry would present. Because of their past involvement in campus ministry, they were committed to a highly relational style of ministry, and they knew that people in their twenties would benefit from forming deep relationships with each other.

They met weekly with Mary while they prayed about it. Together, the three of them formulated a vision and a plan. The Twenties Fellowship was born and grew rapidly. Because of Calvin's location near a major university, there were many recent graduates in the congregation who were looking for connection. Eric and Kim led the weekly group meetings. They organized fun events once or twice a month and planned a camping retreat once a year. In addition to the formal activities, Eric and Kim spent a lot of time with individuals in the group, caring for them and listening to concerns that ranged from spiritual issues to relational questions.

At first they continued to meet with Mary once or twice a month. Kim says, "Mary looked out for us and helped us keep our marriage a priority. She alerted us to what was coming up in the church schedule that we should know about. We were able to brainstorm with her what we were thinking about doing."

Later, for a few months, Eric met regularly with the senior pastor. After Kim and Eric had been leading the group for three years, however, the senior pastor left to take another position, and Mary was unable to resume meeting with Eric and Kim because of extra responsibilities caused by the pastor's leaving. They labored on for another two years. They noticed they were becoming more tired and irritable, and minor relational conflicts within the group became harder to handle.

Kim reflects:

We knew that lots of church groups fail because the leaders are there to have their needs met. So, when we started the Twenties Fellowship, we weren't looking to have our own needs met in the group. I think things started to get hard for us when the pastor left. During the interim period, all the church staff were tired, and it was hard for us to know who to turn to for support. Eric and I were just so tired. We didn't have the resources to work through the conflicts, and we didn't know where to go for help. We were just spent.

After five years leading the group, Eric and Mary reluctantly resigned. They had just become pregnant with their first child. The pregnancy precipitated more feelings of loss for Eric and Mary, as they realized the ministry they had been doing was so disconnected from where they were moving as a couple. The feelings of loss contributed to their burnout.

They stayed on at Calvin, still in close relationships with many in the group. After a few months, Eric's job was transferred to a distant suburb, and they decided to move closer to his work. Commuting to church at Calvin rapidly became too difficult, and they switched churches.

Kim says:

Now I'm volunteering with La Leche League. It's a mom-sized job. They are great at saying, "If volunteering impacts your marriage, quit. If it damages your life, cut back." I've realized we are called to do our job, not another person's job. David wanted to build a temple for God, but God said it wasn't his job, it would be Solomon's. I'm learning to say, "This is what I'm going to do, and that's all I'm going to do."

If I could give advice to churches about how to help people avoid burnout, I would say this: Ask people who are capable to serve in a specific spot, and then don't ask them to do anything else. You wouldn't believe how many things we got asked to do while we were leading the Twenties Fellowship. We got called to work in the nursery, to work on the big cleanup of the church grounds, and to help someone move. We were asked to come to a meeting to brainstorm about adult education classes. It's hard to say no and you feel obligated to help. But it was just too much.

I've been studying the life of Paul and noticing the signs of when it's time to move on. If you're at the height of enjoying things, you aren't open to moving on. But when you start going on autopilot, you risk burnout, but then you're also open to moving on. It's ironic that so often we have to be in some kind of pain to realize the time has come for change.

Recognizing Burnout: More Symptoms

Here are some of the clues that tell me someone is burning out:

- anger, resentment
- obsession with a task—the importance of the task is disproportionate to its real value
- high need for control because they've put so much into a project
- when the project is over, they're gone

—Dan, retired pastor of a large congregation

Patterns of Burnout in Congregations

In many ways, Kim and Eric experienced burnout similar to job burnout. They were exhausted both emotionally and physically. Let us look again at Christina Maslach's list of characteristics of workplaces where people burn out:

- We feel overloaded.
- We feel lack of control over what we do.
- We are not rewarded for what we do.
- We are experiencing a breakdown in community.
- We are not treated fairly.
- We're dealing with conflicting values.[2]

Kim and Eric did not experience lack of control or conflicting values in their service, but they certainly did feel overloaded. They did not mention desiring greater rewards for what they did, but maybe the meetings with Mary and the pastor functioned as a kind of relational reward for them, and those rewards were not available in the interim period when their exhaustion was increasing. Certainly they experienced breakdown in community when the senior pastor left and they no longer had as much support from the church staff. They also felt it was not fair for them to be asked to help in the nursery and with garden cleanup when they were already serving so intensely.

All of these factors added up to an emotional and physical exhaustion that impacted the totality of their lives. The depth of their depletion resembled workplace burnout. In contrast, however, sometimes the kind of burnout experienced in congregations is much more limited in scope. Consider Dena's experience:

> For about 10 years our Bible study group met in our house. We provided the hospitality, and we often led the group. I could tell I was getting sort of burned out. We changed churches, and for the first few years in our new church, we just attended a group. This past year, it met in our home, and it's been good. There's been a kind of healing, and I find I'm ready for that kind of hospitality ministry again.

Dena and her husband experienced a limited kind of burnout and they stopped doing the thing that had burned them out. In fact, they stopped doing it for many years. What Dena left unsaid was the reason they switched churches. Was changing churches a convenient way to get out of a responsibility that had become burdensome?

Was there no other way out? Was there no one helping Dena and her husband listen to how they were feeling about the responsibility of hosting the group? I suspect that changing churches worked as a way to leave the Bible study group without being pressed for too many explanations.

Susan's story gives us yet another viewpoint. Susan still feels deep emotion when she remembers her burnout experience many years ago. She experienced great dissatisfaction during the time she served simultaneously on two boards. On one of them, the church board, the topics for the meetings focused entirely—it seemed to her—on mundane practical issues about the facility, such as purchasing chairs and room use. These topics were not at all interesting to her. On the other board, a seminary board, there seemed to be no interest at all in any kind of change, and she had signed on with the vision of working for change that would make the seminary experience much better for the students. She was bored with the church board and frustrated with the seminary board. Both boards made her angry. She remembers:

> When I was serving on those two boards, no one asked me how I was doing. Eventually I left that church and that denomination for an Episcopal congregation. I like liturgy, candles, stained-glass windows, symbols. The worship feels heart-centered, and my old church wasn't like that. You have to figure out what feeds you and go there. Yet at the same time, life is about service. I have come to believe that we will know when we are serving well because there is joy.

In the three stories I have recounted, one common thread is the serious repercussions of lack of support from the congregation's leaders. In Kim and Eric's case, during their last year years in volunteer leadership the pastoral staff was overloaded because of the departure of the senior pastor, and no one had the time to come alongside them. No one helped Dena think about the cost she and her husband were paying by hosting their home group year after year. No one took the time or effort to ask Susan how she was doing as a board member. Perhaps they did not want to ask because they did not want to hear Dena or Susan talk about their frustration or say they thought they should leave the congregation.

The responsibility to provide this kind of pastoral support for volunteers does not rest only with the clergy in a congregation. Board members and committee chairs need to ask the people who serve in their areas how they are doing and what kind of support they need. They need to encourage volunteers to take personal responsibility to

Hands-On Projects

We recently took a very successful survey. People could not have told us more clearly that they want to participate in hands-on projects that bring them together with others: "Flipping pancakes while talking with people." This illustrates the generational change we're wrestling with. The younger generation doesn't want to chair committees or make long-term board commitments. They want hands-on, finite projects.

—Ben,
rabbi of
a small congregation

get the support they need and to stop serving when the burden gets too great.

In chapter 1, I mentioned Ann, who has served as interim pastor for several small congregations. She has observed that in small congregations, no one wants to mention the word *burnout* because it is too scary to think about losing even a single volunteer. There is always far too much work to do and far too few volunteers. If we talk to people about how they are doing in their volunteer role, they might acknowledge it is too much for them and then we would have more slots to fill.

Yet both Dena and Susan walked away from their congregations after they experienced burnout. Speaker and teacher Malcolm Smith, in *Spiritual Burnout*, writes, "The classic symptom of burnout is to run away from people and be alone."[3] "Running away" in church burnout—whether the congregation is large or small—usually takes the form of changing churches. Dan, retired pastor of a large congregation, says that one of the major symptoms of burnout is "when the project is over, they're gone." Thus, the cost of burnout for congregations is very high.

Burnout in a congregation can impact people's lives so significantly that they experience fatigue and listlessness in all areas of their lives. For others, burnout in their congregation is more localized to just one part of their lives. Either way, all too often the people who experience burnout in their volunteer roles are likely to leave their congregation.

Generational Differences

Many ministers and rabbis told me they have observed that people in the various generations in their congregations approach volunteering with different perspectives. The ministers and rabbis talked about the significant impact of demographic shifts in the past few decades. Because so many women have entered the workforce, one of the most reliable sources of volunteer labor has disappeared. In my own congregation, many mothers of young children do stay home with their kids, but they keep up a schedule of lessons and sports activities for their kids that would have been unimaginable a generation or two ago. And so in many churches and synagogues, paid staff are now performing tasks that used to be done by volunteers.

Another shift seems to have occurred. Several ministers and rabbis, along with other congregational staff members, reported to me that people in the younger generations are interested in hands-on service

40

most of all. They enjoy shorter commitments in ministries where results are rapidly visible. One rabbi in the Midwest said, "People in their thirties will sign up for tasks, but they don't want to do the heavy lifting on committees. They are reluctant to chair committees. When they do serve on boards, they don't engage in the complex issues in the same way that older people do. They don't want to take on long, complicated projects." Thus, the shift in the way the younger generations view service has mixed implications for congregations.

I have observed that younger members of my own congregation enjoy serving in the food bank, which we house for the neighborhood; our weekly dinner, which feeds more than 150 people each week; our children's and youth programs, and the music ensembles, which lead the praise music in worship services. We are a congregation of about 500 in worship every Sunday with a median age under 40, and we have well over a hundred people serving in those hands-on ministries I listed. We have fewer committees than we have ever had, in part because people just are not interested in gathering to talk about nuts and bolts. I would guess that the total number of people on committees is around 25. Even counting elders and deacons, fewer than 50 people attend regular church meetings, while up to 150 people are serving in hands-on ministries.

Ordained ministers, rabbis, and church staff members also reported a notable difference among the generations in their attitude towards burnout. Several people told me that in their congregations, people over 60 continue to serve no matter how they feel about it. They grew up in a time when there was more time to spare, and they are used to volunteering without thinking about how they are doing personally as they serve. People under 40, on the other hand, are more aware of the dangers and cost of burnout and seem to want to avoid it.

Linda, in her late thirties, and Evan, in his early forties, illustrate this trend. They belong to a tiny congregation with a missing generation. Because of the demographics in the neighborhoods near the church, everyone in the congregation is over 70 or under 45. In their 10 years in the congregation, Linda has served in just about every role. She has been a deacon and a worship leader, and she has helped with coffee hour and memorial services. Evan has majored on the church finances and currently serves as church bookkeeper. Linda says:

> The younger people at church watch out for each other. We say to each other, "You look tired. Maybe you need a break from what you're doing." The older people just don't understand it. They keep serving no matter what.

Recently our congregation's annual meeting was scheduled for Martin Luther King Jr. weekend. It was Evan's and my 10th anniversary, and it was a three-day weekend, and we decided to go away for the weekend. So we missed the annual meeting. The older woman who helps Evan with the finances was very critical of our choice. But we've been at every annual meeting for 10 years! And we had just helped with the receptions for two memorial services. We knew we were tired and needed to get away.

People under 40 are not immune to burnout. Eric and Kim's story at the beginning of the chapter illustrates that reality. Younger generations' increased awareness of burnout comes at the same time that everyday life continues to increase in pace and complexity. Even if members of the younger generations in our congregations are more aware of the possibility of burnout, the demands of daily life are great. Many of our congregation members are close to exhaustion just because of the pace they live.

Using Church as a Drug

Between the strong work ethic held by many of the older members of our congregations and the fast pace of life for many of the younger members, a large number of people in our congregations are used to pushing themselves pretty hard. And that can have serious repercussions.

In *The Overcommitted Christian*, Pamela Evans writes that "much of what passes for Christian fervor is workaholism with a religious gloss. Workaholism doesn't just affect people in their place of work. Leisure activities, worship and Christian service can also be affected by drivenness."[4]

She goes on to ponder why we act as if God is interested in competitions and appearances. God knows we need sleep and rest. Why don't we? She asks, "Is it possible that we're being driven beyond God's call, using church to take our minds off the unease or pain that others dull with drinking, drugs, extramarital sex or loud music?"[5] Our culture continually tells us that pain can be dulled with more activities, so it makes sense that people of faith would expect their congregations to be places where they can keep busy and thus feel better about themselves.

Most of the people who talked with me about their burnout experiences came away from that burnout with the conviction, "I won't let that happen to me again." They have now identified some of the forces within themselves that push them towards too much activity for too long. While some of them felt angry that congregational leaders did not do enough to reduce burnout in the congregation, people who have experienced burnout know that they can take steps themselves to make sure it does not happen to them again.

Evans talks about abusive systems as another cause of burnout and as another way that people use church as a drug. She defines abusive systems as families, places of work, churches, groups, and organizations of any sort with a key feature that "individuals do not feel free to think their own thoughts, feel their own feelings, or know what's good for them. There is no true dialogue, and the flow of ideas is in one direction only." In such systems, she says, leaders exercise authority without encouraging people to evaluate teaching and practices for themselves, and participants are encouraged to make sacrifices that are compulsory rather than voluntary.[6] Such a system becomes addictive—like a drug— as congregation members give away their own autonomy and take comfort in the fact that someone else is making decisions for them.

In the light of her definition of an abusive system, congregational leaders will benefit from looking carefully at the way we communicate. Do we encourage evaluation? Do we try to control the spiritual journeys of our members? Do we encourage appropriate sacrifice without manipulation and with affirmation of the need for rest? Do we encourage healthy relationships with limits?

I do believe there is a small amount of abuse in any congregation where volunteers are not being asked how they are doing as they serve. Most likely, the lack of care for volunteers comes either from obliviousness on the part of congregational leaders or fear that asking "how are you doing?" will make the volunteer stop doing their job. Or perhaps the congregational leaders themselves are working so hard that they have no current awareness of the need for balance and rest and therefore do not think to ask about others' well-being.

Physician Frank Minirth and his cowriters in *Beating Burnout* emphasize the significance of an event in Mark 6. Jesus sends out the twelve disciples two-by-two to preach and cast out demons. When they return, "The apostles gathered around Jesus, and told him all that they had done and taught. He said to them, 'Come away to a deserted place all by yourselves and rest a while.' For many were coming and going, and they had no leisure even to eat" (Mark 6:30-31).

Jesus listened to the disciples' report and saw that in the midst of so much activity, they would not get the rest they needed after their strenuous efforts. So he invited them to come away with him to a quiet place for rest. Minirth and his coauthors write:

Causes of Burnout

As I get closer to retirement, I see things more clearly. I've seen the same things in congregations cause burnout over and over:

- lack of visibility and praise for some jobs
- the job turns out to be much harder than people expected or were told
- poorly run meetings
- people hope to do something different or creative, but the way the congregation is structured won't let them
- asking people to do the same things over and over
- power cliques that keep new people from being involved
- unrealistic expectations of what the church can do

—William, associate pastor in a large congregation

That incident highlights an important principle for employers, supervisors, and Christian leaders. It is often easy to become so concerned with "getting the job done" or "doing it right" that we lose sight of the needs of the people who are actually carrying on the work. . . . Our Savior displayed a type of personal concern and compassion needed today when He said to His disciples "Come with me by yourselves to a quiet place and get some rest (or 'rest a while,' KJV)" (Mark 6:31). He sensed that the burnout factor was present in them, so, although there was a vast number of people still unreached, He instructed them to take a break. A close examination of Christ's brief statement shows there are three key elements that, when combined, can relieve the stresses that lead to burnout. These are (1) a change in location, (2) a change in activity or responsibility, and (3) a certain amount of time.[7]

Over and over Jesus modeled his own need for rest and time alone in prayer, so he was inviting the disciples to participate in something he valued in his own life. If congregational leaders are going to be able to uphold and encourage volunteers as they serve, the leaders themselves must have a personal experience of the limits of serving and the needs for rest. And we must welcome the kinds of questions and reflection that keep us from being abusive as we oversee volunteers.

Unstated Expectations and High Ownership

People who are highly invested in only one part of a congregation's life can be prone to burnout. Sometimes we call them "pillars" of the congregation, and the weight of carrying that heavy load can exact a great price. Negative experiences, such as criticism about their ministry area, can be particularly painful for them because their identity is so closely related to the area of congregational life where they are so heavily invested.

Ron, senior minister in a large congregation, believes that people's unstated expectations often lie behind burnout in congregations. In the case of "pillars," they expect that their viewpoint and convictions will be respected because of the amount of time they put into serving. They expect that criticism will be minimal because their hard work must be visible to all.

Ron cites two additional examples of the way unrealistic expectations get people into trouble. He remembers an elder who was assigned to oversee a very practical area of church life. As the months went by, Ron could see that the elder was a relational person who should have been assigned to a different area. Ron kept intervening, saying things like, "This job isn't fitting you. You're not doing a bad job, but the tasks you are taking on appear to be difficult for you. I'd like to help you find a place to serve in an area that suits you more."

The elder never responded to Ron's invitations to change because he expected to fulfill his commitment in the way it was originally stated. He ultimately left the church because of burnout. This burnout incident was partly about the elder's expectation about keeping a commitment. It was also about the congregation's failure to help people identify their gifts, to ensure a good match in the first place.

Ron cites a second example, the way youth directors (and other staff) suffer from expectations that were not laid out when they were hired. He has seen this issue arise several times in the hiring of youth directors. The stated expectation is for the youth director to be a relational person. The underlying, unstated reality is that a tremendous amount of administration is required in youth ministry. After some time passes, and the administrative tasks are not getting done, the church tells the youth director in effect, "We said we wanted you to be relational but what we really need is someone gifted in administration."

Several people who burned out in congregations and came away wiser told me that they are much more careful now to clarify expectations before they take on tasks. Surely congregation members can do a better job asking questions before they agree to serve, but in many cases, congregational leaders need to do a better job articulating expectations as well.

Staff Members

Unstated expectations are just one way that staff members in congregations experience stress. Someone recently told me about the youth worker in her congregation who burned out after two years. This youth worker was expected to work 55 hours each week, similar to the number of hours worked by the full-time ministers in her congregation. But unlike the ministers, she only got two weeks of vacation a year because she was not "professional staff." Her situation is not uncommon.

Staff members in congregations can be subjected to high stress for many reasons. Short vacations, long workweeks, and low pay are certainly one cluster of issues. Lack of clarity about expectations can be deadly, as it was for the youth directors who were asked to be relational while also being expected to be good at administrative tasks.

Overload and lack of control over daily decisions also contribute to the stress. Many congregational staff members have little autonomy in how they use their time each day because they are responsible for responding quickly to the needs of the ministers or rabbis. In addition, they must be civil, supportive, and encouraging to congregation members who ask for their help.

And perhaps the most stressful thing of all is that they cannot complain about any of these stressors or take action to promote significant changes. They are serving God in their jobs! Because their jobs represent a connection to their own faith values and the good of the congregation, they often feel a huge responsibility not to express any of their own needs.

One could argue that some of the same issues affect many ministers and rabbis: overloaded work weeks, low pay, and the inability to realistically meet their own needs because they are expected to serve God without complaining. While it is true that burnout among clergy is a significant issue, support staff in congregations usually have shorter vacations, no opportunity for study leave, and much less control over what they do each day than clergy. Few secretaries, for example, get to come into the office and decide they have just "had it," and then take off to play a game of golf. Many congregational leaders are aware that ministers and rabbis find it easy to overwork in a way that can lead to burnout, but most leaders are not aware that the possibility of burnout among support staff is just as significant as for ministers and rabbis.

Preventing Burnout: Sabbath Keeping

In the first chapter we heard from two people who believe that the cause of burnout is not necessarily insufficient rest but, instead, an orientation towards work where heart motivations and grace are neglected and ignored. How can we rediscover the messages our heart is teaching us? How can we experience grace more readily in all we say and do?

In my interviews, I heard more about Sabbath keeping as a burnout-prevention strategy than any other single idea. People need to allow themselves to rest, and observing a Sabbath is an effective and straightforward way to learn to rest. Sabbath keeping is a biblical practice that, in one sense, is easy to do. When hearing the vague suggestion,

"You should rest more," people have a hard time knowing where to start. Understanding Sabbath rest is easier and clearer: one day each week is set apart to stop working and enjoy God's gifts.

Veteran Sabbath observers say that a weekly Sabbath provides an immensely helpful opportunity each week to grow in learning to live by grace, from the heart. How can we listen to our hearts if we do not have time to do so? The Sabbath gives us time to slow down and listen to God and hear our inner voices. The Sabbath teaches grace, because for one day each week we do not have to be productive. It is enough, on the Sabbath, to be a child of God and to rest in God's care and provision for us. Keeping the Sabbath helps me not only on that day, when I am resting, but during the other six days of the week, when I look forward to that day. It changes the way I experience every day.

In some settings, the biggest obstacle to Sabbath observance may be theological. My husband and I have been observing a Sabbath for 22 years, ever since we returned to the States after living in Israel for 18 months. In Israel, we experienced the Sabbath to be a huge gift, a time with reduced options and a much slower pace, a time of luxury and abundance. Each week we lived a rhythm of six days of productive work and one day of rest, an opportunity to act out the reality that we are dependent creatures of a loving Creator.

When we returned to the States, full of enthusiasm for this practice that seemed to us to be a wonderful gift, we got opposition from almost every quarter. "There's no need to observe a Sabbath any more," people told us. "Our Sabbath rest is fulfilled in Christ." "Observing a Sabbath is legalistic," others said. We stopped arguing and quietly began our own Sabbath observance. It has been one of the significant blessings of our lives. More than anything else in our lives, the Sabbath has taught us grace.

Now, 22 years after we began our own Sabbath observance with no support from anyone, both Christians and nonobservant Jews are rediscovering the joys of the Sabbath. Maybe we simply need it more because our culture is going faster and faster. Maybe we have grown far enough past the Victorian Sabbath rules that made the Sabbath a legalistic burden with no fun allowed. Whatever the reason, I am delighted there are so many helpful books on Sabbath keeping and so much wider acceptance of the need for a weekly rhythm.

How can congregations encourage Sabbath observance? Sermons, classes, and newsletter articles can begin the process of educating the congregation about the joy of the Sabbath. Different Sabbath models can be presented: sunset to sunset on Friday and Saturday, sunset to

Bigger Is Not Always Better

So often we are victims of our success. We do something well, and then we assume we should make it bigger and better. We keep adding things without ever stopping to say, "Can we do all this and still honor the Sabbath?" Our need to make things bigger is idolatrous. It's part of a demonic theology of works righteousness that permeates our culture.

—Mark, pastor of a small congregation

sunset on Saturday and Sunday, all day Sunday, or some other day if a person's work week includes work on Saturday and Sunday. Sabbath observance includes deciding what to eliminate—work, media, housework, or shopping—as well as deciding what will be the focus of the Sabbath time—family games, reading poetry, walks, bike rides, other recreation, or simply doing nothing.

Reducing the number of Sunday meetings in churches can demonstrate a commitment to that day of rest. Talking about the Sabbath as a gift to be enjoyed in our hurried culture can help people understand that Sabbath observance is not just one more thing to do for people who are probably already doing too much. The word *Sabbath* means "stop." The Sabbath is not one more thing to do; it is an opportunity to stop doing so much.

Perhaps the most significant way churches can encourage their members to keep the Sabbath is for ministers and congregational leaders to model it. Do we really believe God's call to a weekly rhythm of work and rest? Do we really believe that we live by grace? Do we really believe that exhaustion is not the best mark of whether we are serving God appropriately? Observing a Sabbath is a great way to face up to the beliefs that permeate our culture that who we are is what we do, or that doing is more important than being. The Sabbath is a huge gift of grace waiting for us to stop long enough to learn from it.

Committees Becoming Communities

In addition to the Sabbath as a practical way to reduce burnout, building teams and fostering community can also be helpful. Dan, retired minister of a large congregation, believes that churches are unique, different from businesses or even other kinds of charitable institutions, in that churches have a commitment both to ministry and productivity, to both building community and getting things done. The best way to model this dual commitment, he believes, is to do our best to transform committees into communities.

At the church where he most recently served, all the committee chairs were encouraged to begin their meetings with a "check in" time, where committee members are invited to share briefly how they are doing in their personal lives. "The worst thing that could happen," Dan says, "is that a committee member has just lost their dog or their job and no one knows. It would be terrible if someone experienced a great loss and no one on the committee knew what the person was going through."

Committee chairs usually resist this idea, saying, "We don't have time for that. Our business takes up the whole time allotted for the meeting." Dan notes, however, that the business of the committee can be handled much more quickly if people feel that they have been heard. Personal sharing at the beginning of the meeting usually eliminates the dynamic of people inappropriately talking on and on about an issue simply because they need to talk. He has observed that when committees become communities, they end up getting a lot done and, in addition, members also feel that someone cares.

Dan believes that building community should be a priority that carries over to congregational board meetings. Personal sharing, perhaps in pairs or groups of three or four, can help people unload the stresses of their life and focus more effectively on the topic of the meeting. Some other kind of spiritual content or teaching—one person's faith story each meeting, a Bible study or lesson, a prayer time for a specific need in the congregation, or the study of a book chapter by chapter— can help board members remember the purpose of congregational ministry. Again, he has observed that the nuts and bolts get done much more quickly when people have already had an opportunity to talk about significant issues.

Over the years, having served several large congregations, Dan says he has heard time and again from staff members, "How can we get church members to do things?" He decided to respond to them, "After three years of working with an elder or committee member, I want you to ask, 'What have I done to this person?' I want you to try to nurture them, shape them, influence them, so that after three years of serving they are more in love with Christ and more committed to Christ's mission than they were at the beginning. This is an opportunity to shape a life rather than use a body up and deplete their energy."

Ron, another pastor, says that he tells new elders, "If it turns out that this role really doesn't fit you, I want you to say so. I will want to talk with you about it—is the role challenging and hard in a good, growing way, or is it not a match? If it's not a match, then I want you to feel free to resign. I want to say up front that being an elder is not for everyone. If it undermines your relationship with God and your relationship with the church, then it is an act of discipleship to quit."

He emphasizes to his elders that the church is both an institution and an organism. He uses the body as a metaphor: both the skeleton and the flesh are part of the body. The institution is like the skeleton and the organism is like the flesh. He says to his new elders, "Some of you are bone people and some are flesh people, and we need both on the board. There will be tension between the two, and we need to keep talking about it." He believes that part of what prevents burnout is an open conversation. People burn out because they do not feel heard.

Mark is another minister who has made a significant effort to build committees and boards into communities. He believes that another key issue in the transformation is for a congregation to become mission driven rather than committee driven. Leaders need to be able to say, "Our core mission is this." That allows board members and committees not to take on responsibilities that do not fit the core mission. Having an understanding of the congregation's core mission also allows the committees to work together with each other, instead of being isolated bodies that focus only on performing certain tasks.

The same need to build community carries over to task-oriented, hands-on kinds of service. In chapter 1, we heard about Christ Church, where many of the volunteers are overloaded and discouraged. The two areas of church life where there is not a lot of burnout—a weekly women's shelter and a soup kitchen—are the places where volunteers get together to share personal needs and pray for each other before they do anything for anyone else. The volunteers receive personal support and experience community as they serve.

Elizabeth, a children's ministries director at a large church, works very hard to build teams of people to work in the various children's classes. She will pair two young married couples or three single women together to teach in a certain age group. She tries to match people who she thinks might become friends as they work together. She believes working in teams reduces burnout for two reasons. Teams enable people to look forward to coming to serve because they know they will be supported as they give, and the team members can back each other up so they can get away occasionally for a weekend and not feel trapped by their commitment to serve.

Elizabeth also encourages the people in leadership in children's ministries to ask the volunteers who work in their area as often as possible, "How are you doing? How can I pray for you?" She believes that kind of personal support goes a long way towards helping people feel supported and cared for.

Building community in committees and hands-on service groups helps people serve from the heart and experience grace. If, as we serve, we are able to talk about how we are feeling, we will be more likely to stay in touch with what our hearts are telling us as we serve. If we experience personal support and encouragement as we serve, we are more likely to bring our whole selves to our serving and find grace in the midst of the hard work. As one church staff person said, "This is not rocket science. It's just people getting together to listen to each other and pray for each other, and then serve others. It's very simple, really." It may be simple, but it takes intentional effort to believe—and then act on that belief—that the relationships formed as we serve are just as important as the service.

The ministers who talked with me about transforming committees into communities mentioned two books that have been helpful resources: *Transforming Church Boards into Communities of Spiritual Leaders* by Charles M. Olsen[8] and *Turning Committees into Communities* by Roberta Hestenes.[9] Both books explain how and why building community in committees and boards makes a significant difference, embracing both relationship and the performance of tasks. While Sabbath keeping was the most common practical idea in my interviews for avoiding burnout in congregations, building community while getting things done was also mentioned quite frequently. As more people live alone, work longer hours, and race from one commitment to the next, we need to offer the possibility of meaningful relationships in places where people serve, including committees and task forces. One rabbi described it as "flipping pancakes while talking with people"—service and community together.

The Two-and-a-Half-Hat Rule

Another way to approach the tendency of people in congregations to work too much or in unhealthy ways is to create structures to put limits on service. Bruce came to Immanuel Church, a small congregation, as an interim pastor. The congregation was active in several ministries. Too many people were serving in two or three or even more church ministries. So he began promoting a slogan: "A job for everyone and everyone with just one job."

The hardest nut to crack was a woman approaching 80 who was washing dishes for coffee hour every week, teaching Sunday school, and serving on several committees. "After several months," Bruce says, "I was able to convince her to drop all but one committee and to retire from teaching Sunday school. She won't stop washing dishes, but I feel good that she isn't running herself ragged every Sunday."

Another church leader talked to me about the "two-and-a-half-hat rule." No one in a congregation, according to this clever slogan, should wear more than two and a half hats. The first hat is a leadership position, the second hat is participating in some other activity regularly but not as a leader, and the half hat is occasional participation in yet a third thing. People can certainly wear fewer than two and a half hats, but no one should wear more. This slogan makes clear that when

Passing on Negative Feedback

I believe one significant cause of burnout is the unnecessary passing on of negative feedback. Recently in our parish there was a big project that lots of people worked on. The person in charge got some negative comments, and she dumped all the negative stuff on the people who helped with the project. Why couldn't she have kept it to herself or talked with the priest? Some of my friends worked on that project and they were so disheartened by hearing the negative feedback. It's the job of the person in charge to be positive and encouraging to those who help.

—Linda, member of a mid-sized congregation

people are involved in three areas of congregational life, they should not be trying to lead all three areas, a helpful reminder for people who feel compulsively responsible for everything.

Elizabeth, the children's ministries director mentioned earlier, said that when she invites an active volunteer to take on new responsibilities, she asks them what they will quit doing in order to make space for this new commitment. Her slogan is, "If you add something, let go of something." She does not want to pile one task on top of another for the people who volunteer with children.

In a congregation with a strong work ethic, these slogans may help members evaluate their service. There will always be something more that needs doing. But one person cannot meet all the needs, and congregations need to help members understand that reality.

More Ways to Provide Structures to Limit Serving

In addition to limiting congregation members to one or two and a half areas of service, term limits can be helpful. Dan, the retired pastor of a large congregation, believes that committee members should have limited terms of service. In one congregation he served, a certain committee had many members who had been involved for decades. New people would come to the committee, attend one or two meetings, and then stop coming. When he asked them why they stopped, they could not point to anything specific. No one was rude or unwelcoming, but there was a vague feeling that no one new was needed and that the old guard had things under control.

In Dan's denomination, elders and deacons serve three-year terms with the option of continuing for a second term. He believes churches will have less burnout when committees adopt the same structure. Records need to be kept of when a person joins a committee, and new committee members need to be informed that six years is the limit for staying on any committee.

In our congregation, with so many young people, no one is interested in maintaining the kind of structure that tracks how long people have served on committees. But it is still worth considering how open our committees are to welcoming new people or if an "old guard" has developed that controls the committees. Perhaps some of these long-time members might need a break.

Another practical idea that can help with preventing burnout is to provide regular opportunities to assess spiritual gifts. Whether a congregation uses the spiritual gifts passages in the New Testament or personality type inventories like the Myers-Briggs Type Indicator or the Enneagram, classes and retreats that help people explore and articulate human differences can help people understand that not everyone should serve in the same way. This emphasis on individual differences can give people the freedom to begin to follow their heart into service rather than do what they feel they should do.

In my own congregation, we offer a spiritual gifts seminar each year and, as a part of the seminar, we give people the opportunity to begin to think about a personal mission statement. We ask them to answer the question, "If I could do one thing for God without fear of failure, it would be . . ." One woman reported several years later that completing that statement was a turning point for her, and she took significant steps to act on the words she wrote. Helping people acknowledge their inner dreams, passions, and desires will help them serve with increased joy because they are acting from their values, from their heart.

Community and Task

Truly, congregations are an odd blend. We are called to accomplish tasks: provide worship services, care for our children and youth and others with special needs, and reach out into our communities. We are called to be an oasis of spiritual health for our members in the midst of their demanding lifestyles. We are called to be different from our culture and to serve within it. In order for congregations to be healthy, all of these things have to be held in tension and somehow embraced all at once.

Congregations become systems that promote burnout when they focus too heavily on tasks and forget the bigger purpose. That is why working to build committees into communities is so effective; it helps committee members remember that they are here to be more than a task force. That is why Sabbath keeping is so significant; the Sabbath helps us remember that we are called to experience grace as well as get things done. That is why having a congregational mission statement can be helpful; boards and committees can put their work in the context of the larger purpose.

The spiritual health of our members is paramount and must always be considered, even when the volunteer pool is painfully small and the tasks seem overwhelming. Otherwise, we are in danger of forgetting who we are, called by God to live and serve in communities of joy, called to honor God with worshipful work.

4
INDIVIDUAL DIFFERENCES
ON THE ROAD TO BURNOUT

There are varieties of gifts, but the same Spirit; and there are varieties of services, but the same Lord; and there are varieties of acivities, but it is the same God who activates all of them in everyone.

—1 Corinthians 12:4-6

One of the greatest gifts of my life has been my marriage. One of the gifts of my marriage has been the fact that my husband, Dave, and I are such different people. We are a good example of the reality that opposites attract. I have lived for more than half my life with a man who enjoys and receives energy from different things than I do, who is stressed by different things than I am, and who is renewed in different ways than I am.

And, after 26 years of observing the significant differences between us, I know deep inside that people burn out for different reasons. We are not all alike.

Dave loves to serve in hands-on ways. When he sees someone with a practical need, his heart fills with love and he longs to be able to help. He is innately a great listener and cheerleader. He is able to give people encouragement and acceptance almost as easily as breathing (it seems to me—I have to work at those two skills). He is stressed when he has to deal with abstract things, too many administrative details, and particularly when he has to do things that do not involve people either directly or indirectly.

As I said, I am very different. My greatest joy is learning something—the more abstract the better—and then teaching it to someone else. I love to read, think, design curricula, write, teach, and speak. I enjoy talking with people one-on-one about life issues, but I have to concentrate to be a good listener. One of the most stressful things I ever have to do is to help someone in a hands-on way.

Over the years we have learned ways to exercise and have fun together, so we can spend time off with each other. But, if left to ourselves, we relax and wind down from stress differently. My most basic coping strategy involves being alone, and Dave's involves activity with people, particularly something physical. Being alone for a long block of time soothes my soul deep inside. The same hours alone would feel stressful to Dave. I find physical activities with groups of people to be highly stressful and not soothing at all, while Dave is energized and relaxed.

If, like many researchers, we consider burnout to be caused by too much negative stress coupled with too few coping strategies, we need to consider the ways different individuals are stressed and the ways they learn to cope. I have seen very clearly in my marriage that the very activity that will cause discomfort and stress to one person will be a positive, energizing challenge to another person. I have seen very clearly that one person's coping strategy is another person's stressor.

If we consider burnout to be an affair of the heart caused by serving and working in ways that do not fit with our values and motivations, we need to consider individual differences in heart motivations. Again, I can see clearly that the deep heart motivations of one person will leave another person cold. We are not all alike. In fact, our differences are amazing and striking.

In this chapter we will look at three ways to describe individual differences: the spiritual gifts list in Romans 12, personality type as described by the Myers-Briggs Type Indicator (MBTI), and the Enneagram. These three ways of describing human differences give us language to talk about stressors, what being stressed looks like, coping strategies, and inner motivations.

I love to find positive and encouraging ways to describe human differences. So often we think that deep down other people must be just like us or mostly like us. Of course, in many ways, humans are alike: we have many of the same longings and deep needs. But at the same time, significant individual differences among people give spice to life and help us reflect God's image in different ways.

As we look at these three ways of describing human differences, we will focus particularly on the ways different people experience stress, find effective coping strategies, and identify the heart values that will guide them into effective ministry. These are foundational issues as we consider the different ways volunteers in our congregations burn out.

Lack of Support for Where Our Hearts Lead Us

I was not being nurtured at church, so I decided to try to find programs that would feed me and might feed others. I began a particular Bible study program at church that I enjoyed very much. I got no support for it. No one said we shouldn't do it, but they also didn't support it. I was hurt by the lack of support for the Bible study program I began. When you do what your heart leads you to do, and people don't accept it, it hurts.

—Susan, congregation member

The Spiritual Gifts List in Romans 12

In the New Testament, the apostle Paul lays out various kinds of spiritual gifts in three major lists, in Romans 12, 1 Corinthians 12, and Ephesians 4. A number of writers and scholars believe that the three lists present different kinds of spiritual gifts. Don and Katie Fortune, in their book *Discover Your God-Given Gifts*,[1] provide the best descriptions of the Romans 12 gifts that I have found. These seven gifts, which the Fortunes call "motivational gifts," are a great place to start when trying to explain the different ways people are motivated from within to serve. These gifts can help us identify the patterns of serving that come from our deep motivations. We will be more joyous in our service and less likely to burn out if we are serving in ways that come from our inner motivations.

In fact, when I am asked to teach a church-related class or group something about individual differences, I usually use the Romans 12 gift list rather than Enneagram type or Myers-Briggs type, even though I have written a book on the MBTI. The seven gifts described in Romans 12 are easy to understand, and people can easily get a sense of where and how these gifts are used consistently in congregational life.

Here are the verses from Romans:

> Having gifts that differ according to the grace given to us, let us use them: if prophecy, in proportion to our faith; if service, in serving; the one who teaches, in teaching; the one who exhorts, in exhortation; the one who contributes, in liberality; the one who administrates, with diligence; the one who does acts of compassion, with cheerfulness. (Romans 12:6-8, my own translation)

When I teach about these gifts, I always start with the easiest to understand, service, and work my way to prophecy, which is the most complex to explain. As I describe the Romans 12 gifts, I will draw heavily on the descriptions in the Fortunes' book.

Service is probably the gift we see most often. People who have the gift of service like to help others in practical, hands-on ways. Both my husband and my mother have this gift. You are likely to find my husband taking meals to people who are sick, helping someone move, or helping our grown sons with car repairs. My mother serves on the altar guild at her church, and she enjoys washing and ironing the exquisite altar linens. She also fixes food for church dinners and takes care of neighbors' cats when their owners are on vacation.

Compassion, or mercy, is another gift we see often. Just like the person with a gift of service, the person with the gift of compassion has a heart for someone in need. A server will want to meet practical needs, while a person motivated by compassion will likely express an emotive kind of caring, perhaps by asking questions about how the person is doing and listening to the answer with great sensitivity. The compassion person may draw out the person in need, asking more questions and encouraging the person to talk some more. Or they may sit in encouraging silence. In this kind of attentive listening, love and care will be communicated.

Exhortation or encouragement, on the surface, appears to be similar to the gift of compassion because both involve words that communicate acceptance. But the compassion person will be listening and accepting in a nondirective way, while the exhorter will be trying to move the person in a certain direction. An exhorter might say, "Go ahead, try! I know you can do it. You've got the skills and the motivation. Go for it!" The exhorter uses words to motivate people to act in ways that help them grow.

The *administrator or leader* also uses words to motivate people to act, but the administrator's concern is not so much for individual growth but for the smooth functioning of a group of people to accomplish something. The administrator likes to oversee people and tasks. A good administrator wants to see people serving where they will grow and develop, but he or she is most concerned about accomplishing a purpose.

The *teacher* is, first and foremost, someone who enjoys learning. Teachers will often have their noses in books or will be gathering information as they talk to people. Teachers usually have a passion for truth, objectivity, facts, accuracy, and words. This is my primary spiritual gift, and nothing gets me more excited than knowing I have understood something well enough to explain it clearly, so people can grasp the main idea and some of the nuances as well.

The *one who contributes, the giver,* is a person who sees what is needed and enjoys giving it. Givers are generous with money, possessions, time, and energy. They enjoy giving high-quality gifts, and often enjoy hospitality. Many givers enjoy giving anonymously and have no need for recognition for their gifts.

Prophets are people who see things differently than other people, so the Fortunes call them "perceivers." Perceivers see good and evil more clearly than other people do; in fact, they are often accused of being black-and-white thinkers. They see God's hand at work, and they are quick to recognize evil. They are perceptive about what is going on inside people and within groups. We think of prophets in the

Bible as people who speak out what they see. Don and Katie Fortune emphasize that the first calling of the prophet is to prayer. Only after much prayer should prophets speak the truth that they see.

Many people have a cluster of gifts they use most often, and the way the gifts work together influences what they look like. My mother's gift of service is coupled with a gift of administration, while my husband's gift of service is coupled with compassion. My mother serves in an efficient, organized, and scheduled way, and my husband serves in a more spontaneous, behind-the-scenes, listening-oriented way. The way the various gifts work in combination with others creates a multi-faceted community reflecting God's glory in countless ways.

When I teach about these gifts to groups, I use two practical examples to illustrate what the gifts look like. First, I describe a scene at coffee hour. I tell the group that a little boy is running across the room holding a cup of juice, when he trips over a wrinkle in the carpet and falls down. I ask them to imagine that seven people rush over to help. Each person has a different one of these Romans 12 gifts. What would each person do?

- The compassion person would probably kneel on the floor, hold the boy's hand, ask him if he's OK, and listen carefully to the answer.
- The server would clean up the spilled juice.
- The exhorter would pick the boy up, hand him a fresh cup of juice and say, "This time I'm sure you'll do great."
- The teacher might say, "See, now you know what happens when you run with a cup of juice."
- The administrator might be standing there organizing the various people who came to help, or the administrator might be thinking about what it would take to fix the carpet.
- The giver would either get a new cup of juice or think about giving the money to replace the carpet.
- The prophet or perceiver would likely be standing back watching the situation. The perceiver might have watched the whole thing happen, noting that the boy had been teased by his friends, causing him to run across the room in frustration. Or the perceiver might be carefully observing the dynamics of the group helping the boy, noticing the people who seem to be helping out of love while others are helping because of a need to be needed. Whatever the perceiver sees, it is likely beneath the surface of what others are seeing.

A second scenario that I ask people to consider is a team of people who are teaching Sunday school for elementary school children. If there are seven people, each with one of the gifts, what will they want to do?

- The server will probably be in charge of snacks or room setup.
- The compassion person will enjoy sitting with the one child who feels left out and needs special attention.
- The administrator will want to organize the schedule.
- The exhorter will probably enjoy teaching elementary school children more than the teacher will, because so much of teaching children involves encouragement, not communication of facts.
- The teacher will probably enjoy choosing curriculum.
- The giver will probably want to bring the snacks or crafts materials.
- The perceiver will probably notice the individual needs of certain children, and the perceiver will be invaluable at evaluation time, when the groups gets together to debrief and talk about what really did happen of significance in the classroom.

We will see when we get to the Myers-Briggs Type Indicator that experts have made two suggestions about what causes burnout: working too much out of one's strengths and working too much using one's weaker areas. From my observation, the same seems to be true when we consider spiritual gifts as well. If someone with gifts of administration and teaching spends a lot of time doing dishes and helping people in need, she is likely to get very tired. If she continues to serve, over and over, in ways that push her to use only her weak areas, she may burn out.

In contrast, imagine that this person with gifts in administration and teaching is constantly arranging retreats, teaching classes, planning curriculum, and scheduling other teachers. She is very, very good at all these things because her gifts are continually being used to their fullest, so she gets invited to do more and more and does it all. Burnout could be around the corner for her, also, because we need to spend some time doing things that are difficult for us, so we can grow and so we will live with balance in our use of strengths and weaknesses.

I believe we are called to use all of the spiritual gifts from time to time, and that a healthy pattern of ministry will involve a great deal of time using the gifts we do have and small amounts of time using gifts we do not really have. A simple way of describing this idea would be: When we work only out of our strengths, we are not growing, but when we work only out of our weak areas, we are not doing what we were created for.

Table 4.1
Symptoms of Stress: The Romans 12 Gifts

When we approach burnout, the very characteristics that were good and admirable in us become warped and twisted into something negative. When under stress . . .

- Servers can feel unappreciated, critical of those who are not helping, and unwilling to accept help themselves.

- Compassion people tend to become indecisive, easily hurt, and overly sensitive to others' needs.

- Teachers tend to become intellectually proud, legalistic, and dogmatic.

- Exhorters can become dogmatic and overly outspoken about what someone else should do.

- Administrators tend to become callous to people's needs, driving others or "using" them to accomplish goals.

- Givers may become erratic in their giving or controlling around how their contributions are used.

- Perceivers tend to become judgmental, blunt, and intolerant, unable to see anything positive.

Adapted from *Discover Your God-Given Gifts* by Don and Katie Fortune

---

These Romans 12 spiritual gifts can help people figure out how best to serve in the ministry areas they feel strongly about. Identifying which Romans 12 gifts we have will not tell us whether we would rather serve with children or youth or seniors or with the soup kitchen. We have to identify our own interests and passions to know *where* to serve. But once we pick a place to serve, understanding these gifts can help us know *how* to serve.

Identifying these gifts will enable us to make better choices as we take on tasks and say no to others. Understanding these gifts can also help teams work together better. Congenial relationships among those who are serving together goes a long way to prevent burnout, so identifying our own gifts and the gifts of those we serve with can help prevent burnout by building community. If we identify gifts in our committees and teams, we can operate as a "body"—noticing how every member is different but necessary.

Myers-Briggs Type

Many people have taken the Myers-Briggs Type Indicator at work or in their congregation. Some people have identified their type by taking a variety of other tests, some of them on the Internet, that have been developed in recent years to assess this kind of personality type. I will give a brief overview of MBTI type and then present the implications for burnout.

Carl Jung's book *Personality Types* was translated into English in 1923, and a mother-daughter pair was immediately fascinated by it. The mother, Katharine Briggs, had been studying personality for years, and she found in Jung's book a theory that addressed many of the questions she had been considering. The daughter, Isabel Briggs Myers, took Jung's ideas and began to write questions to help people try to identify their type. She felt an increased urgency during World War II, because she observed that so many people were taking on war work that they were not suited for. During the 1940s and '50s she assembled questions, tested them to make sure they were statistically valid, and the Myers-Briggs Type Indicator was born. It underwent a major revision in the late 1990s.

The MBTI reflects Jung's theory of personality. Jung observed that people do two things with their minds. First, we take in information, or perceive. Second, we make decisions about the information, or judge. Jung believed that there are two ways of perceiving and two ways of judging, and that each person prefers one over the other.

Jung called the two ways of perceiving "sensing" and "intuition." When we are using "sensing," we stay with the information from the five senses. When we use "intuition," we make a leap from sensory information to something else: an abstraction, a metaphor, an image, or a pattern.

Jung used the words "thinking" and "feeling to describe the two ways of making judgments or decisions about the information received. When we use "thinking," we employ logic to evaluate information. When we use "feeling," we focus on values in making the decision. These values usually include the impact on people that will result from a decision.

These four things that the brain does—sensing, intuition, thinking, and feeling—are called "functions." Everyone uses all four of them at various times.

Some of Jung's vocabulary is unfortunate. "Judging" or making judgments (decisions) sounds like it involves being judgmental, but that is not the case. Jung uses judging simply to refer to the process of making a decision. "Intuition," as Jung uses it, also bears little resemblance to the way we talk about intuition in common parlance. He uses it to describe an abstract process of taking in information in contrast to receiving only sensory information. And when Jung uses "feeling," he is not referring to human emotions or feeling. He is using it to contrast with thinking, using logic to arrive at a decision. "Feeling," in type language, means being focused on people and values rather than impersonal logic as we make decisions.

Jung believed that everyone has a preference for either sensing or intuition and for either thinking or feeling. He also observed that

---

Table 4.2
The Basics of Psychological Type
(from the Myers-Briggs Type Indicator)

Attitudes

Source or Direction of Energy	Outer World	Extraversion (E)
	Inner World	Introversion (I)

Functions

Two Ways of Perceiving	Five Senses	Sensing (S)
(Gathering Information)	Leap to the Abstract	Intuition (N)

Functions

Two Ways of Judging	Analytical Logic	Thinking (T)
(Processing Information)	People Values	Feeling (F)

Attitudes

Orientation to the Outer World	Desiring Closure	Judging (J)
	Keeping Options Open	Perceiving (P)

---

everyone uses these four functions either in the outer or inner world. That's where the language of extraversion and introversion come in. If people use their most preferred function in the outer world, we call them extraverts. If they use their most preferred function in the inner world, we call them introverts. Introversion and extraversion indicate the source or direction of our energy. When we are receiving energy from the outer world, or directing our energy towards the outer world, we are using an extraverted function. When our energy is received from or directed to the inner world, we are using an introverted function.

Extraverts are usually more comfortable with large groups of people than are introverts. Introverts are usually more comfortable with small groups of people or with time alone. We need to be careful not to overgeneralize here, because a good number of extraverts are quiet and reserved people, and a good number of introverts are outgoing and social. The issue is where we are most comfortable directing our energy or receiving energy: the inner or outer world.

Isabel Briggs Myers and Katharine Briggs observed that people prefer to use either their perceiving function (sensing/intuition) or their judging function (thinking/feeling) in the outer world. That is where the fourth letter of the MBTI comes from: the preference for the judging or perceiving function in the outer world. People who prefer judging generally feel comfortable with schedules, deadlines, organization, structure, and policy. People who prefer perceiving usually prefer open-ended processes and flexibility, and they are often energized by last-minute tasks and decisions.

Jung used the analogy of being left or right handed to help people understand the kind of preferences that type describes. Everyone who has two functioning hands uses both of them, but almost everyone has a preference for their right or left hand. There are a few people who are ambidextrous or close to it, but most people have a clear preference for one hand over the other.

When we think about type and burnout, this hand imagery can help us understand what is going on. As a right-handed person, if I overuse both hands about equally, my left hand stops functioning first. In fact, when I had carpal tunnel syndrome about 15 years ago from too much typing and piano playing—both of which use my hands about equally—it was my left arm that gave out first. That was where I had the most pain. The muscles simply are not as well developed on my left side because I am right handed. Carpal tunnel is like burnout, caused by too much stress and too little relief. For me, carpal tunnel problems come from overusing my less preferred hand.

If I write too long with a pen, however, my right hand gets knotted up and stops working effectively. My right hand becomes less accurate, and I have less control. I have, in effect, burned out my right hand from overuse of a part of my body that is quite competent and easy for me to use. In fact, I am so comfortable using it that I forget to notice when it is getting tired.

Researchers on type and burnout have theorized that burnout can come either from overuse of our most preferred function or from overuse of our least preferred function. There does not appear to be any data about whether one or the other is more common. A balanced life seems to involve using our most preferred functions most of the time, while using the other functions from time to time, so we grow, develop, and have inner balance. Overusing either our most preferred functions or our least preferred function sets up some kind of emotional strain that can lead to stress and burnout.

One British researcher, Anna-Maria Garden, did some fascinating work on what burnout looks like for different types. She found that people who prefer sensing become less able to deal with details when they are burning out, and people who prefer intuition become less able to consider the big picture. She also found that people who prefer feeling become harder and less sensitive to the needs of people, and people who prefer thinking become less analytical and more concerned about people.[2]

I have heard anecdotal evidence that confirms Garden's research. I have heard about people who are concrete and factual (indicating a preference for sensing) who begin to catastrophize under stress and imagine all sorts of negative possibilities that bear no relation to the facts. Some people who are big-picture thinkers (with a preference for intuition) become obsessed with insignificant details under stress. I have heard stories about people who are analytical and unsentimental (indicating a preference for thinking) who become sappy and overly emotional when under stress.

Much of the research on workplace burnout indicates that as people are burning out, they become less sensitive to the needs of the people around them. Garden's research would suggest that this would be most true of those who prefer feeling. Since much of the burnout research has been done on people in the caring professions, where a preference for feeling is most common, it makes sense that researchers would observe that the majority of the subjects become less caring. According to Garden, however, people with a preference for thinking can actually appear to be more caring as they approach burnout.

Another significant area of research on type and burnout involves the question of whether some types burn out more easily or more often than other types. This kind of research involves determining if some types experience more stress than other types and also if some types use more coping strategies than other types.

The research shows that introverts experience more stress than extraverts and feeling types experience more stress than thinking types. (Regarding stressors, the research shows there is no difference for the sensing/intuition or judging/perceiving preferences.) If introverts and feeling types experience more stress, does that mean they burn out more often, too? Yes and no. Research indicates that introverts do burn out more than extraverts because introverts, on the average, do not have and use as many coping strategies as extraverts.

In contrast, the research indicates that feeling types use many more coping strategies than thinking types, and evidently those coping strategies compensate for the increased stress that they experience. According to the research available now, thinking and feeling types' burn out at pretty much the same rate, even though feeling types experience more stress.[3]

In one seminar I led on type and burnout, I had a vivid illustration of the abundant coping strategies of extraverts and feeling types in contrast to introverts and thinking types. It was a very small seminar with only six participants. Two of the participants had type preferences of INTJ, three had preferences for ENFJ, and one for ENFP. I put the two INTJs together and the other four (with ENF in common) in another group and asked both groups to list the coping strategies they enjoy using.

The two INTJs—one man and one woman—talked for a long time before they wrote anything down. Ultimately, they decided, their major coping strategy when under stress was to work harder to get the job done. Getting finished removes the stress, so they always push on to get done with whatever was causing the stress. They also noted that walking was a good stress reliever for them, so they might occasionally take a walk when under stress and enjoy the beauty of the world. Ultimately, they ended up with two things on their list of coping strategies: continuing to work and walking.

My own type is INTJ, and I watched with amusement while my two seminar participants spent so much time talking about how they like to get a job finished before they can relax. I could see myself reflected in them, and I recognized the risk I run for burnout all the time because of my high need to finish things. I came out of that discussion more committed than ever to continue the growth process of learning when to set aside my perfectionism and my need to finish.

The other group—two men and two women with preferences for extraversion, intuition, and feeling—wrote a list of more than 20

Table 4.3
Symptoms of Stress for the 16 Myers-Briggs Types

ISTJ— excessive emphasis on precision, high need for control

ISFJ— pessimism, lack of emotion, stinginess, become demanding and overly conventional

INTJ— skepticism, broader questioning, obsessed with hair-splitting precision

INFJ— increased caution, unrealistic expectations, pessimism about the world

ISTP— become restless, critical, overly analytical, obsessed with feelings of rejection

INTP— become restless, defensive, rebellious, hypersensitive, and disappointed in others

ISFP— become undependable, suspicious, hypercritical, skeptical, and touchy

INFP— become touchy, unrealistic, distracted, impulsive, critical, and petty

ESTP— become opportunistic, restless, unkind, engage in catastrophic thinking

ESFP— seem to be undependable, touchy, rigid, abrupt, engage in catastrophic thinking

ENTP— become impulsive, unrealistic, hasty, ask for answers very forcefully then later become very quiet

ENFP— become impulsive, hasty, distracted, very talkative then later very quiet

ESTJ— become demanding, instructive, hypersensitive, seen as aggressive, arrogant, and stingy with resources

ENTJ— become aggressive, arrogant, hypersensitive, detached, high need to get the job done now

ESFJ— engage in hasty observations, unrealistic expectations, and nit-picking

ENFJ— internally self-critical and can appear pushy, impatient, hasty, impulsive, and hard-headed

Adapted from *Enhancing Leadership Effectiveness through Psychological Type* by Roger Pearman coping strategies they use at different times. When stressed, they might talk on the phone or have lunch with a friend. They might take a bubble bath, light a scented candle, do something artistic, or listen to music. They wrote down several ways to enjoy nature and get exercise: walking, biking, hiking, gardening. They might get a massage or treat themselves to a manicure.

This group ran out of space on the piece of paper that I gave them. To me, this was a clear illustration of the reason why introverts burn out more than extraverts, and why feeling types do not burn out more than thinking types, even though feeling types experience more stress than thinking types. I could see clearly the ability of feeling types to understand how and where to receive personal nurture when things get tough.

Type can also help people notice and describe the stressors they experience:

- Introverts often experience stress in large groups or when having to cope with the outer world for long periods of time.
- Extraverts often experience stress when they have to be alone for a long time or when they cannot think out loud about what they need to do next.
- Sensing types often experience stress when they have to deal with abstract concepts or undefined tasks for a long time.
- Intuitives often experience stress when they have to deal with concrete details for long periods of time.
- Thinking types often experience stress when dealing with people needs.
- Feeling types often experience stress when the emphasis is on a task or information, with no consideration for relational harmony or other people-related needs.
- Judging types often experience stress when they have to keep things open-ended for a long time.
- Perceiving types often experience stress when rapid closure is necessary.

Type can also help us to articulate and explore the kind of coping strategies we enjoy. For example, extraverts often use coping strategies that involve relationships, and introverts often use coping strategies that involve being alone or with only one person. In considering coping strategies, however, the situation is more complex than it first appears. If the most effective coping strategies help to bring balance to our lives, then extraverts who work with a lot of people will need time alone, and introverts who work alone will probably need time with friends.

Earlier I mentioned the seminar where I had two groups of people list their coping strategies. The extraverts listed lots of coping strategies that involved being alone; in fact, the majority of the coping strategies on their list were solitary activities. All of them worked in people-intensive jobs, so it was no surprise that they experienced balance through recreation that involves being alone.

A mature understanding of type does not put ourselves or other people in boxes ("I'm an extravert, so I can't be alone"). Type is most useful when we understand that we will use all type preferences from time to time, just like we use both our right and left hands. The language of Myers-Briggs type can help us articulate our preferences and less preferred areas of functioning. Type can help us notice overuse of either our strengths or weaker areas, so we can avoid the stress and burnout that comes from that kind of overuse.

Enneagram Type

The Enneagram is another way of describing personality differences. It involves nine different personality types arranged on a star. I have read different accounts of the origin of the Enneagram. Some experts say it is based in ancient Sufi teaching; some say it came from South America. It appears to me that no one knows for sure where the Enneagram came from. We do know, however, that several decades ago, Catholics began using it as a tool for spiritual growth.

There is no validated test or indicator for the Enneagram like there is for Myers-Briggs type. Several of the books on the Enneagram have different inventories to help people discover their type. Not only are these inventories different, but each writer describes the nine types differently, even using different names for the various types. It can be frustrating to try to master Enneagram type because of the diversity of the ways people write about it.

Why mention it at all if there is no validated instrument or consistent body of knowledge about it? I find Enneagram type to be helpful because it gets at the same basic issue as the spiritual gifts list from Romans 12—our motivations—but goes deeper. Enneagram type helps us see the dark side of the things that motivate us, and thus it can help us move towards significant growth.

When discussing different patterns of burnout among different people, the Enneagram does several things. It can help us understand the kinds of settings in which we might burn out, and it describes

Appropriate Recognition

Laboring when no one really notices kills volunteering. Conversely, overrecognition of someone in a high-profile volunteer position leads to cynicism on the part of other volunteers. Genuine appreciation is essential and difficult to achieve.

—Deanna, member of a mid-sized congregation

pretty vividly what approaching burnout will look like for different people. Like the Romans 12 gifts, the Enneagram can help us understand how to serve in ways that draw on our deepest motivations, which will help us prevent stress and burnout.

The Nine Enneagram Types

A variety of names are used for the Enneagram types,[4] and each type can be expressed in both healthy and unhealthy ways. Some people function in healthy ways most of the time, some are unhealthy most of the time, but any individual can be healthy one moment and unhealthy the next. When we are under stress, we are more likely to move into the less healthy manifestations of our Enneagram type.

1. The Perfectionist or Reformer

Primary motivation: to do a good job, do things right, crusade for justice

A healthy One works hard, carefully doing what is good or right, with integrity and wise judgment. An unhealthy One is perfectionistic, thinks his or her way is the only way, and can be rigid, anxious, intolerant, or resentful.

2. The Helper or Giver

Primary motivation: to serve, care for, love and protect others

A healthy Two gives and serves selflessly in a variety of settings. An unhealthy Two needs to be needed, moving towards codependency, approval-seeking, people-pleasing, and inability to access true feelings and needs.

3. The Motivator, Achiever, or Performer

Primary motivation: to be a success, to make a good impression, to perform

Healthy Threes motivate themselves and others to develop their potential to the fullest. An unhealthy Three needs to be the center of attention and can become workaholic, narcissistic, vain, and exploitive of others.

4. The Tragic Romantic, Artist, or Spiritual Alchemist

Primary motivation: self-actualization, to be original, special, or unique, to give meaning to pain

A healthy Four is characterized by creativity, empathy, and a deep awareness of spiritual reality. An unhealthy Four can feel self-hatred, envy, isolation, and be obsessed with pain and death.

5. The Thinker or Observer

Primary motivation: to understand

A healthy Five loves to study, ask questions, formulate theories, and enjoys the knowledge and wisdom they have accumulated. Unhealthy Fives might be isolated, insecure, and stingy, blocking all emotions and denying their own needs.

6. The Loyalist, Trooper, Questioner, or Devil's Advocate

Primary motivation: to feel secure

A healthy Six is loyal, devoted, and socially conscious, enjoying creating security and stability for themselves and those they love. An unhealthy Six can be anxious, fearful of being abandoned, overly dependent yet controlling of the people around them.

7. The Adventurer, Generalist, or Epicure

Primary motivation: to experience pleasure, to be happy

A healthy Seven enjoys the wonder of the created world and is filled with joy, curiosity, adventure, and innovation. An unhealthy Seven can desire excitement at any cost and fall into manic activity, avoidance of feelings, fear of commitment, narcissism, and gluttony.

8. The Leader, Asserter, or Boss

Primary motivation: to lead, to be in charge, to be self-reliant.

The healthy Eight is courageous and fearless in leadership, desiring the best outcome for everyone involved. An unhealthy Eight can be aggressive, contemptuous, deceitful, unwilling to rely on others, full of vengeance and cruelty.

9. The Peacemaker or Mediator

Primary motivation: to maintain peace and harmony

A healthy Nine sees the good in every person and in every situation, and brings peace, harmony, and safety to their relationships. An unhealthy Nine can become immobilized, go for peace at any price, deny problems, be overly accommodating, and struggle with fear, hostility, and anger.

Ways the Enneagram Is Helpful

The appeal of the Enneagram for me is multifaceted. I greatly enjoy thinking about the diversity of people's primary motivations. I believe that understanding these deep motivations when we work with people can help prevent burnout, because we will not push people to serve in ways that violate their deepest motivations. And for ourselves, understanding our inner motivations will help us know when to say yes and when to say no.

I enjoy observing these primary motivations in my own family. As I said earlier, my husband loves to help and serve. He is a quintessential Two. One of our sons is a Nine, and it has been a delight to see the ways he strives for relational harmony. A close relative of ours is a Five, and I enjoy watching the intensity of his constant desire to understand new things.

In addition, the call to spiritual growth within each Enneagram type has been helpful to me in my own life and as I talk with others about their spiritual growth. My Enneagram type is One, and I can see clearly my desire that everything be done well. At my best, I am a hard-working, diligent person who uses all I am and all I have to serve God with my drive for excellence. At my worst, I am controlling, overly perfectionistic, believing my way is best, resentful of anyone who disagrees with me or slows me down. I have the choice in each moment how I am going to express this part of my self.

Understanding this primary motivation of mine, to do things well, has been helpful within my family and within the staff of the church where I work. I can appear bossy, particularly when I believe I know the best way to do something well. I have learned to say to people around me, "My drive is to get things done well. It often looks like I want to do things my own way, but that's really not my primary motivation. Please let me know if you have an idea of how to do things better. I want to hear it. I am not at all married to my own way of doing things."

Before I learned about the Enneagram, I was baffled that people so often perceived me as bossy, when I knew quite well that most of the time I did not have a lot of ownership of my way of doing things. The Enneagram gave me language to describe what is going on inside me. I sometimes look like an Eight, wanting to be in charge, but my deepest motivation is not to do things my way, but to do things well.

I come closest to burnout when I have too many things on my plate, and I literally cannot do them all well, no matter how hard I work. Obviously, I need to grow away from being such a perfectionist. But I also need to be careful, possibly more careful than some other types, not to take on so many things that I have to lower my standards of excellence too much. When I have too many balls in the air, I can exhaust myself trying to get things done to a minimum standard that I can live with.

Table 4.4
Symptoms of Stress for the Nine Enneagram Types

1. The Perfectionist	Work becomes compulsive, pleasure is eliminated from the schedule, fears of abandonment and not living up to high expectations
2. The Server	Increasingly preoccupied with other's needs, personal needs repressed, punishing people for ingratitude
3. The Performer	Moving into hyperdrive, energy spent on trivia, become dependent on relationships but also suspicious
4. The Romantic	Intense feelings of grief and abandonment, small irritations in relationships get magnified
5. The Observer	Become territorial, withdrawn, and isolated; exercise control in a demanding way
6. The Trooper	Tightening of defenses, feeling of dread, fight or flight response, feeling of numbness or excess energy
7. The Epicure	Withdrawal, comparing self to others in the area of pleasure others get to experience
8. The Boss	First, opposition and aggression; then, withdrawal into intellectual pursuits and analysis
9. The Mediator	Paralysis; inactive, armchair depression; obsessive, worst-case scenario thinking, blaming others

Adapted from *The Enneagram in Love and Work* by Helen Palmer

A friend of mine told me about a time when her husband burned out. Her husband is a Three, with a deep desire to achieve or perform. They moved across country so my friend could go to graduate school, and her husband looked for a job. There was a bookstore close to campus that was about to go bankrupt, and he took on the challenge of bringing the bookstore back to life. He succeeded. He greatly enjoyed the struggle and challenge involved in saving the bookstore, and he had resurrected it long before his wife was finished with graduate school. His mistake was to stay on at the bookstore after it had reached the maintenance stage.

He loves a challenge, but he could not take the day-to-day running of the bookstore. Too much routine, too little challenge, and too little opportunity to excel. He became dispirited and discouraged, moving towards burnout. Mercifully, his wife finished graduate school and they moved again, giving him the opportunity for a fresh start. Today he sells real estate, and the varied daily challenges and the new opportunities to achieve and perform keep him motivated and happy in his work.

The Enneagram also describes what happens to people as they move towards burnout. When under stress, Enneagram theory teaches that people first slide downward within their own type. So for me, as a One, stress will first make me more perfectionistic, more likely to be anxious, intolerant, and judgmental. As the stress becomes greater, every Enneagram type moves towards another type. You can see in pages 76 and 77 the direction of stress/lack of health for each type. In fact, the lines within the circle of the Enneagram show the way each type moves towards another type either in health or in stress.

When we move towards another type because of stress, we will express the unhealthy characteristics of that type. So for me, a One, the theory says that I move towards Four in a stressed state. While Four at its best is a spiritual, sensitive, and artistic way of living, when I move towards Four under stress, I am likely to resemble the worst of a Four: self-absorbed, filled with self-hate, and overly focused on death and pain.

Likewise, when I am healthy, there will be a movement towards the good aspects of Seven, and my perfectionism will gain a lightness and freedom to enjoy life. I could never live my life totally as a pleasure-seeker, but I enjoy the overtones of joy and fun that come from Seven.

One of the best known writers on the Enneagram, Helen Palmer, believes that under stress we can also move in the direction of the healthy arrow, but we would manifest the unhealthy side of that type. So if I moved towards Seven under stress, I could fall into manic activity, avoidance of feelings, fear of commitment, narcissism, and gluttony.[5]

The strength of the Enneagram lies in its ability to describe the diversity of human motivation, along with the dark side of that motivation. The Enneagram lays out a significant challenge for individuals to grow in expressing that motivation in a healthy way. All of us can flip amazingly quickly from healthy to unhealthy expressions of these deep motivations, so the Enneagram can give us insight into the people around us as they move in and out of stress. One spiritual director who uses the Enneagram says it is wise to explore it with someone else, someone with whom we feel safe, because few of us are able to accurately identify and honestly explore our dark side. Having a companion makes both more possible.

The nine patterns of motivation of the Enneagram can be helpful for congregational teams to discuss, so people can gain some understanding of what motivates others. Understanding our own Enneagram type can be helpful as we work with others, because we will see more clearly what we are motivated to do and in what ways we need to depend on others. Probably the most significant contribution of the Enneagram for congregational leaders lies in the area of personal humility and the call to growth. As leaders we need to see the ways we are drawn into unhealthy patterns of behavior that damage our relationships with others.

DIRECTION OF HEALTH/SECURITY

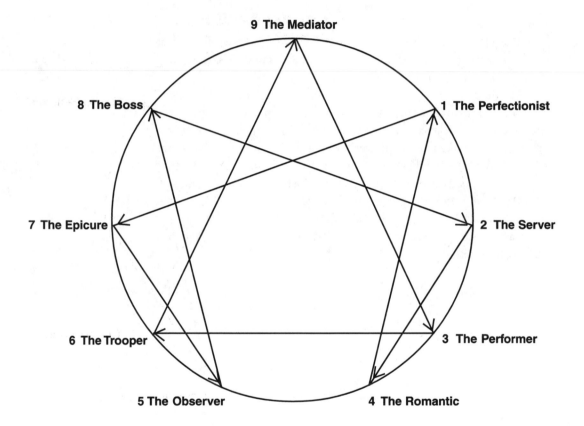

DIRECTION OF STRESS/LACK OF HEALTH

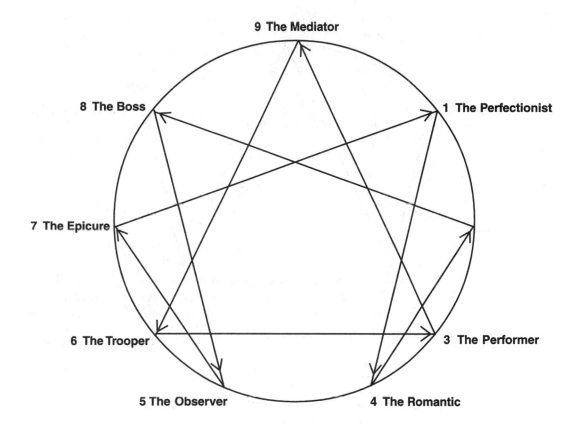

People Are Different

In this chapter, we have seen an overview of three different ways of describing the differences among people. Because this chapter has given only a brief overview, I want to encourage you to go deeper if you are interested. In the bibliography at the end of this book, you will find lists of books on spiritual gifts, Myers-Briggs type, and Enneagram type.

Isabel Briggs Myers had a positive view of the value of describing differences among people. She entitled her book on type *Gifts Differing*, and she was aware of the biblical source of her title: "Having gifts that differ according to the grace given to us, let us use them" (Romans 12:6 RSV). Myers hoped that her work would help people celebrate their own gifts and the gifts of others.

When we respond appropriately to our giftedness, we will be less likely to burn out. We may choose to work outside our area of giftedness for a season, maybe because of a deep passion or commitment, but we can be more aware that exhaustion and stress may result. And we will know that we need relief. We may take on a task that overuses our strengths, but we will know that sooner or later we need to have some balance.

When we learn what stress looks like for our type, we can monitor it more easily. In the previous chapter, I told the story of a couple who reported that the people at church watch out for each other. "Take a break," they say to each other when they observe fatigue and stress. When we know what the buildup of stress looks like in our family members and ministry coworkers, we will be more able to help them take that break when they need it.

We may also choose to ask some questions when we see signs of stress. "Are you serving out of your passion?" "What got you started serving here? Are those same values still significant to you?" "Tell me why you do what you do. What motivates you?" Asking these kinds of questions in a gentle way, with a listening ear, can go a long way towards helping a congregational volunteer or staff member think through whether or not they should continue serving in that way.

The list of gifts in Romans 12 and Enneagram type can help us access some of the forces that motivate us. These motivations will help us discern how to serve. These motivations will not tell us where to serve; we need to consider further what motivates us in order to know where we can serve with energy. Do we have a concern for the homeless, the grieving, the handicapped? Is there an age group that we feel a particular passion for: children, youth, young singles, or seniors?

When we read the newspaper or watch the news, what kinds of human needs leap out at us and grab our hearts? No system of personality type can help us access those kinds of passions, yet it is essential to understand them in order to serve from the heart.

I truly hate the idea that learning about type would put people in boxes or lead people to believe that we have categorized them. Tread lightly if you use type in your congregation. Watch for uniqueness and giftedness in people and rejoice in it, but do not talk a lot about type if people are not open or interested. As I have watched volunteers in my congregation using the lens of these three ways of describing people—without mentioning anything about it—I have reaped great benefit. I have grown in ability to appreciate personal differences and the ways we all need each other. I have been able to ask better questions about personal motivations, sources of stress, and coping strategies. I do a better job of explaining what is and is not important to me.

Maybe only one of the three patterns described in this chapter will seem helpful to you. Maybe all three will. In any case, I hope that you have gained an understanding of the variety of ways that different people experience stress, find coping strategies, and experience deep motivations.

5
COMPULSIVE BEHAVIOR

It's not what you eat that destroys you; it's what eats you.

—Mark Twain[1]

When I was in the middle of researching this book, I had an interesting conversation with my husband's cousin. He is in his midforties and works as a researcher. He is intelligent, dispassionate, and analytical. He loves his work and sometimes works long hours. He has a quite a few recreational interests and takes initiative to do the things he enjoys.

This cousin kept coming to my mind one week as I was reading about burnout and talking with people who had experienced burnout. I realized that I could not imagine him ever burning out. I knew somehow that he would resist job pressure that would move him towards burnout. I knew that if he were ever in a job that required more than he could give in a healthy manner, he would do everything possible to try to renegotiate the job, and if that did not work, he would quit. He is a faithful volunteer at a food bank, and I have never seen him take on more than he wants to.

He does not have one iota of what I might call a "martyr spirit," that drive to keep on working, serving, giving beyond a place that is healthy for the self. He is not self-absorbed or selfish. He simply knows his limits very clearly.

So I said to him the next time I saw him, "I can't picture you burning out. Can you imagine it happening to you?"

He answered, "No." He said that if his job required painfully long hours, he would do it for a month or two, but after that, "I just wouldn't be able to do it." Something inside him protects him against that kind of damage to himself.

Then we talked about what we had seen in people that makes them give so long that it damages them. Why does one person know when to stop and when to say no? Why does another person take on more than they can handle? Why do some people keep on working or serving in menial positions that do not use their gifts and strengths? Why do some people keep on serving long after the joy has departed and they are serving out of sheer diligence?

Physicians Frank Minirth and Paul Meier, along with several other authors, have written a book to answer that question. Their 1990 book on this topic is entitled *Before Burnout*, and it was reprinted together with another of their books on burnout in 1997 with the new title *Beating Burnout*. They believe that there is an obsessive-compulsive element in people who serve until they burn out. In this chapter, I will summarize what they have found as they worked with people who burned out because they simply could not stop serving.

Another answer to the questions listed above comes from researchers on trauma, who look at war veterans and victims of various kinds of abuse. People who experience residual effects of trauma tend to respond in one of several predictable ways. One kind of ongoing response to trauma involves serving mindlessly and endlessly doing thankless tasks that are well beneath the ability level of the person serving. This kind of compulsive behavior may be rooted in past events, and in this chapter we also will look at trauma response and its implications for congregational burnout.

In this chapter, we will look at issues concerning "difficult" people. I also want to look at the role models in congregations and the effect of their modeling. In my interviews, I heard over and over that some congregational leaders model compulsive service in a way that significantly impacts members of the congregation. Those influential congregational leaders can be ordained ministers or rabbis, and they can also be the members of the children's ministries committee or the elders in charge of fellowship.

Obsessive-Compulsive Behavior

Tim was raised in a traditional family. His father, a strict disciplinarian, exercised absolute authority. His mother was quiet and submissive, apparently content to let his father be in charge. Tim was the middle of three children, the only son, and as a young child he fell into the role of peacemaker. He learned that the more invisible he and his siblings could be, the more peaceful the family would be, so he worked very hard at being invisible and keeping his siblings happy so they could be invisible, too. Tim reflects,

> I didn't do drugs or sex. Instead, fixing was my addiction, keeping everyone happy, trying to make things smooth. It worked when I was a kid, so I guess I thought it would work as an adult, too.
>
> At church, the way to fix things and be invisible is to get things done yourself. If I stopped overseeing the church finances and the building repairs, I would have to ask for help, look for someone to take over, and that would make waves and break up the peace. So I keep on doing things, even though I would really love to quit. I just don't know how. It's starting to have an effect on my health. My blood pressure has been high the last few times I've been to the doctor, so I know I need to quit fixing. But I don't know how, really.

Minirth and the other authors of *Beating Burnout* would say that Tim shows signs of obsessive compulsive behavior. In defining these terms, they write, "Clinically speaking, an obsession is a particular thought repeated over and over to the point that it is difficult to dislodge from the mind. Such *obsessions* usually result in frequently repeated behavior patterns. Those are known as *compulsions*."[2]

In its most extreme form, obsessive-compulsive behavior takes the form of agoraphobia, panic attacks, anxiety attacks, inability to sleep, handwashing hundreds of times a day, and other behavior that can greatly interfere with everyday life. Medication, counseling, and even hospitalization might be necessary.

Minirth and the other authors point out that many people exhibit obsessive-compulsive behavior that impacts their life in less drastic ways. The man who frequently pats his hip pocket to make sure that his wallet is still there, and the Sunday school teacher who cross-checks every Scripture reference before class, are manifesting compulsive behavior, probably rooted in obsessive thoughts.[3] Individuals with obsessive-compulsive aspects to their personality are often productive, conscientious workers who get a lot done because they are careful, thorough, and see a job through until it is finished. Obsessive-compulsive behavior is rewarded in many situations, and it can help people achieve their goals in life.

The authors write, however, "Obsessive-compulsive (perfectionistic) behavior can be destructive, both to the obsessive-compulsives and to those around them. Though obsessive-compulsives

Recognizing Burnout: Church Was Where I Worked

When I was burning out, what I felt first was boredom. The church wasn't speaking to me or feeding me, yet I was going to endless board meetings to discuss issues that bored me, like building programs and the purchase of chairs. I became more irritable and annoyed with the mundane issues we discussed and the critical spirit of the people. Finally, I

(continued)

looked elsewhere for spiritual nurture. The church was where I worked, but my spiritual nurture came from my own personal study and the doctoral program I began. Eventually, I left that church and found a different congregation. The outcome of burnout for me was finding a community that is a better place for me, a place of spiritual nurture. I have energy for church again, and I learned that I simply cannot serve in places where people want to talk only about nuts and bolts.

—Susan, congregation member

are unlikely to fail at a job through irresponsibility, carelessness, or neglect, they are likely to bring about a catastrophe by working themselves to the point of burnout."[4]

In *Beating Burnout*, the authors describe two kinds of perfectionism: quantity and quality. In both kinds, the person desires to exhibit *perfect* behavior in order to ensure self-worth. Quantity perfectionists will define *perfect* by looking at the number of things they are involved in. The higher the number, the greater the level of perfection. They will take on 20 things to do in one day, accomplish 19, and kick themselves around for not doing enough.

Quality perfectionists will try to do each thing perfectly. They will not take on a lot, but whatever they do, they attempt to do it absolutely perfectly. Since absolute perfection is difficult to define, they often do and redo tasks, hoping they will hit perfection.

On the outside, quality and quantity perfectionists look different. One is doing way too many things and the other is doing only a few things. But neither achieves "a balance of emphasis (focusing one's time strategically) and breadth (participating in a variety of activities)." To do that they would have to balance the extremes of quality and quantity, which obsessive-compulsives find difficult to do.[5]

I have certainly seen both kinds of perfectionism in congregations. On the one hand, some people seem to be involved in everything. They help teach children, organize the coffee hour, chair the women's committee, and also usher. A quality perfectionist, in contrast, will take on one task and do it to the nth degree.

I believe that Evelyn is probably a quality perfectionist. She has taught junior high Sunday school in her small congregation for more than 20 years. She sends cards to the kids and parents, always has abundant snacks, and spends hours each week preparing the lesson. In fact, long ago she abandoned attending the worship service in order to spend that time preparing for the next class.

Some of the kids feel loved and cared for by her extravagant involvement. Others feel smothered. One of the warning signs of her compulsion is that she does not attend worship or any other church activities where she might receive nourishment. All her attention and identity are focused on performing in her role as teacher.

Minirth and the other authors observe that obsessive-compulsive personality traits are most commonly formed in the oldest child or the oldest boy or girl. They also note that a high proportion of missionaries, Bible college students, pastors, and seminarians they have counseled at the Minirth-Meier Clinic—the majority of whom are firstborns—have obsessive-compulsive personality traits.

84

They cite the story of Mary and Martha in Luke 10 to illustrate the fact that obsessive-compulsives tend to be project-driven rather than motivated by relationships and people's needs. In the story in Luke, Jesus came to Mary and Martha's home for dinner. Martha busied herself with the meal preparations while Mary sat at Jesus' feet. Martha, the gospel writer says, was "distracted by her many tasks," and she came to Jesus and asked, "Lord, do you not care that my sister has left me to do all the work by myself? Tell her then to help me" (Luke 10:40).

Minirth and the others list Martha's obsessive-compulsive traits exposed in this story. They write that Martha

- considered the project of having the Savior for dinner more important than acknowledging the Person of Jesus Christ
- labored far too hard over the project
- would not or could not relax and enjoy the Lord's presence
- preferred working to anything else
- was critical of her sister, Mary (for not helping her), and even of Jesus (for not having encouraged Mary to help her)
- was motivated to control Mary as well as Jesus (to help her control Mary)
- took action that would likely lead to interpersonal conflicts[6]

As a woman who has often felt overwhelmed by the demands of preparing food for guests, I have sympathy for Martha's feelings. I am not sure we can know whether or not Martha has labored far too hard over the dinner she was preparing. I have always wondered if maybe Martha really did need help in the kitchen! I do agree with Minirth and his coauthors, however, that the whining tone I hear in Martha's words indicates she has some kind of problem. She also seems to have a desire to control the people around her. And there is no doubt that her priority was placed on the accomplishment of a task rather than the relationship.

In addition to being perfectionists and focusing on the project at hand, obsessive-compulsives tend to focus on details, dirt, and money. They tend to love in a conditional way, probably because they received conditional love, and their approach to others can lead to competitiveness and power struggles.[7]

Obsessive-compulsives are not likely to be comfortable feeling and expressing emotions. They prefer thinking and doing and working. Underlying the compulsion and the control, significant pools of anger, fear, self-doubt, and guilt may simmer and bubble. They find it hard to face those negative emotions because their perfection would be called into question.[8]

Idealism and bitterness are two characteristics of obsessive-compulsives that have great implications for burnout. Idealism leads a person to enthusiastically plan or endorse a particular project for their congregation. When others prove to be indifferent or simply less enthusiastic, the obsessive-compulsive's idealism is shattered, which can begin the path to burnout. The story that I told at the beginning of the first chapter, about the woman who had great idealism as she started to chair the fellowship committee at her church, illustrates this unfortunate reality.

Minirth and the other authors are convinced that bitterness also plays a significant role in burnout. In their 1987 book *How to Beat Burnout*,[9] they go to great lengths to lay out the power of bitterness to infect people with a kind of poison that leads to burnout. Bitterness seems to result from hanging onto idealism too long, from expecting perfection in people and institutions. Bitterness leads us to believe that no one, including God, understands how hard we have worked and how much we have suffered. We think that life is not fair and we are getting a raw deal.

The only cure for bitterness is forgiveness. The Christian gospel is a message of forgiveness, but for some, forgiveness is easier to talk about than to achieve. Perhaps exposing the poison of bitterness can help people move towards forgiveness.

Responding to Obsessive-Compulsives

How can a person with obsessive-compulsive tendencies lead a healthy life? Minirth and the other authors present the following list:

- First, deal with the current causes of stress. This may mean quitting a job or stopping volunteering in a particular position. For quantity perfectionists, some of the quantity of responsibilities must be decreased.
- Second, deal with physical stress by getting exercise, rest, and a healthy diet.
- Third, realistically assess goals and schedules.
- Fourth, pay attention to the origins of the obsessive-compulsive tendencies. This may well involve counseling.
- Fifth, give up grudges and bitterness and choose forgiveness.[10]

This list will be helpful to the person who is motivated to make personal changes, even though each step will probably be extremely difficult and time-consuming.

What about congregational leaders who see obsessive-compulsive traits in people who serve in their area? What can a congregational leader do to help?

First, we have to affirm that ultimately we can do nothing to change another person. We can create congregational structures that limit certain behavior. We can listen to people and try to understand the forces that lie behind their behavior. We can encourage the person to receive counseling or quit a particular place of service or to adopt a particular healthy behavior. We can teach about God's unconditional love. We can teach principles of healthy service, including information on spiritual gifts and God's call to joy as we serve. We can come alongside people when they do burn out, helping them to see the repercussions of obsessive-compulsive behavior. We can pray for people who push themselves too far. But we cannot change other people, and we must not expect that we will be able to.

When I interviewed clergy and lay leaders, asking them how they respond when they see people exhibiting compulsive behavior within their congregations, the answers clustered in two major areas: structural and relational.

Some congregational leaders believe that the only strategy that has any hope of helping reduce compulsive behavior involves structural changes that limit everyone's service in healthy ways. Term limits, where all leadership and committee positions last only for a stated period of time, make certain that no one can get overly focused on one area of service. A congregational policy that everyone should be involved in only one ministry can help quantity perfectionists. A more realistic variation, the "two-and-a-half-hat" policy—everyone can lead only one thing, be a regular participant in one thing, and be an occasional participant in something else—can encourage people to let go when they do too much. A sabbatical policy, where everyone in leadership takes a year off from significant responsibility when their term ends, can help people to experience congregational life without the need for compulsive service. Teams of people serving together can reduce the extreme ownership that sometimes accompanies quality perfectionism.

Other congregational leaders talked to me about the ways they deal with compulsive behavior in a relational way. In chapter 2, I told you Sister Sylvia's story. She burned out as principal of a Catholic high school, largely because of her need to do everything perfectly. I asked her what she would do if she saw someone serving with the same

---

Recognizing Burnout: Do You Need Permission to Pull Out?

My role as shepherd is to keep an eye on people's well-being. When I see things that make me suspect burnout is coming, I have a direct communication with the person. I say, "Here's what I see. Do we need to give you permission to pull out?" Burnout is like a headache; it's a symptom of something going on. These are some of the things I watch for:

- avoidance and procrastination, either individual or collective
- communication with a subtext of "I feel resentful," which could be in jokes, asides, complaints, or even in body language
- the words "I feel burned out," which is the healthiest response

—Mark, pastor of a small congregation

kind of compulsive drive towards perfectionism that she manifested before burnout. Sylvia answered,

> I would sit with that person and ask her to talk about her story. I really believe that overextension often reveals a deep need, the need to be noticed or appreciated. Sometimes something difficult is happening at home. So I might say, "You've been so generous with your time here at church. Tell me what your everyday life is like."

A sensitive leader will listen, spend some time thinking and praying about the story, and maybe consult with someone else in leadership. Ultimately, the leader may need to say very gently, "I think you're doing too much." We have to be so careful saying that because the person usually has a bruised and damaged sense of self. We do not want them to think that God is rejecting them in some way because we are suggesting that they serve less.

Our goal is to help the person find one task that would help her develop a talent and feel chosen, a niche where the person can serve in a sincere way and spend quality time without being overextended.

Other questions that leaders can ask people who are serving compulsively include: Are you getting joy and satisfaction from your serving? How is your relationship with God or your personal spirituality impacted by your serving? In what ways have you experienced the presence of God's Spirit as you serve?

Asking these kinds of questions is not going to solve anything quickly, but the questions serve as a reminder that joy in serving, spiritual growth, and the experience of God's presence with us are part of what people can expect when they are serving in a good place in a healthy manner. Over time, if people hear often enough about joy and growth and heart and grace in serving, it may have an impact that moves them toward a more healthy attitude in their serving that does have obsessive-compulsive aspects to it.

As we ask questions and listen, we need to be attentive for an underlying message of "God will love me more if I do this." The desire to earn God's love through faithful service shows an inadequate experience of the love of God. When we hear this reality in someone's words, we can gently say something like, "God loves you already." And we can watch carefully to see that none of our words or actions reinforce the idea that God's love depends on our actions.

We must remember that the obsessive-compulsive personality traits we have been discussing usually do not disappear overnight. They are often deeply rooted and powerful. We can create structures to limit unhealthy behavior and we can ask questions, listen, and pray, but we must be patient and remember that we can never change another person.

Trauma and Its Results

Minirth, Meier, and the other authors of *Beating Burnout* do not spend a lot of time addressing the issue of where compulsive behavior comes from. They mention that it is most common in oldest children or the oldest boy or girl. They mention that people who show compulsive behavior often did not have emotionally close relationships with their parents. But that is as far as they go in suggesting a cause.

I have seen in several cases that people who experienced abuse are prone to compulsive behavior that leads to burnout. And when I read a book called *The Betrayal Bond*, I began to understand more of this dynamic at work. The author, Patrick Carnes, is an expert on addiction and recovery and has written several books on addiction. In *The Betrayal Bond*, he explores the kinds of compulsive behavior that come from trauma and betrayal.

First, he describes the kinds of situations where trauma or betrayal might happen: domestic violence, dysfunctional marriages, exploitation in the workplace, religious abuse, litigation, kidnapping, hostage situations, cults, addiction, incest, and child abuse.[11] Then he describes three different kinds of trauma. Some kinds of trauma are intense within a short time period, such as rape, an accident, an assault, and one-time incidents of child molestation. One of my friends fell off her roof while cleaning the gutters, and she exhibited classic signs of post-traumatic stress syndrome for a year or so after the accident.

Some kinds of trauma are relatively minor, but they happen every day, and the hurt and damage accumulates. Ongoing child neglect, a toxic marriage, or a toxic job would fit this second category. Carnes writes, "Little acts of degradation, manipulation, secrecy and shame on a daily basis take their toll. Trauma by accumulation sneaks up on its victims."[12] The compromises we make in coping with these minor kinds of traumas can deaden us over time.

The third kind of trauma, major and long-lasting traumas, are, of course, the worst. Torture victims and prisoners of war suffer for many years. Victims of ongoing child abuse, incest, and domestic violence experience intense trauma over and over again.

Carnes identifies eight patterns of response to trauma:

1. trauma reaction: when we experience the trauma over and over even though it has ceased
2. trauma arousal: when we use high-risk behavior (such as sex, drugs, gambling) to cope with effects of the trauma
3. trauma blocking: when we anesthetize ourselves with food, drinking, eating, compulsive working, or exercising
4. trauma splitting: when we split off a part of ourselves through fantasy, "spacing out," compartmentalizing our life, even amnesia
5. trauma abstinence: when we deny ourselves basic human needs and simple luxuries
6. trauma shame: when we feel we should be punished for what happened, which often results in loneliness, estrangement, and self-mutilating behavior
7. trauma repetition: when we continue to place ourselves in situations where a similar kind of trauma will occur
8. trauma bonds: when we recreate the trauma in some form for ourselves or others[13]

Several of these kinds of responses have implications for congregational burnout. Trauma blocking can manifest itself in someone who works hard to cover over the pain, often working at jobs or serving in positions that are well below the person's abilities. Engaging in trauma abstinence can make a person feel that they should not receive anything good, including rest from labors. Trauma shame, with its self-destructive behaviors, can motivate a person to serve and serve, especially when it hurts. And trauma repetition pushes people to return to difficult situations where people take advantage of them.

What makes these behaviors happen? In *Trauma and Recovery*, psychiatrist Judith Herman explains the fight or flight response that happens in trauma. The ordinary human response to threat involves a complex biochemical reaction beginning with increased alertness and ability to focus on the threat, ignoring other needs. She writes, "These changes in arousal, attention, perception, and emotion are normal, adaptive reactions."[14]

When the fear is intense or lasts for a long time, "the whole apparatus for concerted, coordinated and purposeful activity is smashed. The perceptions become inaccurate . . . the sense organs may even cease to function. . . . The functions of the autonomic nervous system may also become disassociated with the rest of the organism."[15] These alterations of consciousness that happen in trauma often have lasting effects. Victims of trauma report ongoing feelings of numbness, "shutting down of feelings, thoughts, initiative and judgment."[16] Herman calls this "constriction," and she says:

This narrowing applies to every aspect of life—to relationships, activities, thoughts, memories, emotions, and even sensations. And while this constriction is adaptive in captivity, it also leads to a kind of atrophy in the psychological capacities that have been suppressed and to the over-development of a solitary inner life. [17]

In other words, chronically traumatized people no longer have a baseline state of physical calm or comfort.

It is no wonder, then, that people who have experienced trauma might work or serve long after they are exhausted. If their ability to perceive their own needs has atrophied, they simply will not know that they are working too long. If they have no sense of their baseline state of calm and comfort, they will not know when they have pushed themselves beyond it for too long.

In our congregations, we may have people who are still experiencing some kind of post-traumatic stress disorder because of military service in a war. We may have people who have been kidnapped or raped. The most common kind of past trauma I see in my own congregation is sexual abuse dating from childhood, the teen years, or early adulthood. The trauma from sexual abuse can affect both men and women. It can lead to many different kinds of self-destructive behavior, including excessive serving beyond the point of health.

In addition to the severe kinds of trauma that result in a person's inability to notice and respond to their own needs, I have also seen milder forms. Let me tell you Christy's story to illustrate a more subtle trauma response.

Christy was a dreamy, introspective child who loved to read and draw. Her parents both had powerful personalities with strong opinions about what kids should be doing, and their priorities did not include reading and drawing. Her dad loved sports and thought the discipline of sports was the most important thing for both boys and girls. Christy was a klutz at sports. Her mom was socially active and wanted her daughter to love clothes and parties and the social whirl like she did. Christy was shy and never felt comfortable in social settings.

Christy tried to measure up to her parents' expectations, but she knew she continually embarrassed her mother and disappointed her father. She often felt incompetent, like she had been made wrong. An assortment of common childhood traumas—teasing, classroom jealousy, the theft of some of her personal possessions at school—affected her deeply, in part because she did not feel she could tell her parents how upset she was.

Burnout and Love

I think John 15:13 speaks to burnout: "No one has greater love than this, to lay down one's life for one's friends." Burnout happens when we lay down our life, but we have long ago stopped loving. Love is the only real and lasting motivation that enables us to lay down our lives in a healthy manner. Without love, we dry up, we blow up, we burn out. This echoes the first three verses of 1 Corinthians 13. It is of no use to give our bodies to be burned, Paul says, if we don't have love.

—Christina, seminary student

Christy came out of childhood into adulthood bruised and battered, even though she had never been abused in the technical sense of the word. As an adult, Christy struggles with some of the same issues that affect people with post-traumatic stress disorder. She feels out of touch with her body and its needs, she has a hard time knowing when to stop working, she is not very good at resting or playing in ways that rejuvenate her, and she sees herself engaging in self-destructive behaviors that she cannot stop doing.

I can see clearly how Christy's upbringing caused her to believe over and over that her own perceptions were wrong and that she could not trust her own desires or needs. In that way she is like a trauma victim. When Christy reads the literature of trauma, she identifies with many of the symptoms, yet she can see clearly that her parents loved her and had the best intentions as they tried to lead and guide her. She feels that she had so much more privilege in her childhood than true abuse victims, so she sometimes feels that she should not have been so strongly affected by her childhood.

Responding to Trauma Victims in Our Congregations

I Am Not the Savior

People who burn out tend to hold things too tightly, unable to let go—dying with their hand to the plough. When I see them I want to say, "Let go; remove yourself from the high need for significance." I am not the savior of the world. There is a lightness that comes from not believing I'm essential.

—Ron, pastor of a large church

I made up this story you have just read about Christy. I based it on stories that I have heard frequently over the years from both men and women. I believe that most congregations have people like Christy. They are often quiet, hardworking volunteers who are very sincere in their faith. Their involvement in their congregation is often precious to them, because they find in their faith the acceptance and love they crave.

They can easily tend towards overfunctioning in their serving, because, like victims of more intense trauma, they often find it difficult to believe they should care for themselves, and they are often out of touch with their body and their emotions. Sometimes, they literally cannot feel when they should stop. They may choose to serve in ways that underuse their gifts and talents because they have an inadequate view of what they have to offer. And yet their faith and their involvement in their congregation is a lifeline for them.

How can congregational leaders respond when we believe that a volunteer might have been a victim of some kind of trauma, whether large or "small"? What can we do that would be helpful?

Beyond structures that limit everyone's serving in a healthy manner and careful listening, we can also encourage therapy, prayer for inner healing, and support groups. I have observed that people who experienced ongoing trauma in the past, whether low-key like Christy's or much more intense, heal slowly from the trauma. Sometimes there are giant steps forward, but usually the progress is very, very slow.

As we work with people in our congregations who are walking along the healing road, we need to have patience with their progress, allowing them to move forward at their own pace. We may see bold and bright talents in a person who systematically hides them. It may be very obvious to us that someone is serving in a place that does not use his gifts very well. Yet that place of invisible or menial service may be the only place where he feels safe. We can give gentle encouragement, affirming the gifts we see, but we must not push people who have been wounded too far beyond where they feel comfortable.

Likewise, when we see a vulnerable person serving too long and too hard, we can encourage the person to rest and play, but we have to realize that we simply cannot change another person. We cannot force someone towards healing.

We also need to realize that we can invite people to tell us their story, but they may not choose to do so. I loved Sister Sylvia's gentle approach to asking people about their lives: "You've been so generous with your time here at church. Tell me what your everyday life is like." Over time, trauma victims may feel confident to share the story of their past. But they may not. And even when they do tell us, that will likely be only one very small step towards healing.

As we deal with people who are overworking in our congregations, we need to realize that often a significant wounding lies behind the compulsive behavior. We need to tread gently with everyone, because we do not want to injure the wounded any further.

"Difficult" People

It would be easy for a cheerful, upbeat person who works in a volunteer position with someone like Christy to believe that she is "difficult," one of those problem people who make things hard for church staff and leaders. After all, she seems to need more care and attention than other people in the congregation.

Someone like Christy who is very sensitive and needs gentle interactions might get labeled "difficult." People who are demanding in a variety of ways might get that label, such as lay leaders who are very controlling, those who have high standards for the ministry they are involved in and who demand a lot from staff and participants, people who have a high need to talk a lot, people who are impatient and want things done now, or those who come into a congregation with a preexisting bias against the church, clergy, or some aspect of congregational life.

Two books published by the Alban Institute do a great job describing the challenge of caring for people who seem to be difficult: *Never Call Them Jerks* by Arthur Paul Boers[18] and *The Care of Troublesome People* by Wayne E. Oates.[19] Both books emphasize the necessity of looking at the whole congregational system, and both books help the reader learn how to provide care for people who exhibit difficult behavior. Both books encourage congregational leaders not to talk about difficult *people*, but rather to focus on *behaviors* that are challenging to cope with.

People like Christy often do require more attention and care than some other volunteers. In the midst of meeting their needs, we need to remember the purpose of congregations. We do not exist only to run efficient children's ministries programs or stellar adult education classes. We are primarily in the business of helping people grow in faith. Our role as congregational leaders will involve trying to be sensitive to the needs of people who require extra gentleness and care.

In addition, we will from time to time need to establish and maintain boundaries around what we will and will not do to support volunteers who serve in our congregations. Sam, a youth director, talked to me about a particularly demanding volunteer in his program. For many years, this woman had taught one of the youth Sunday school classes. She had a high level of ownership of the class, and she had extremely high standards of the way the class should be run. She also had high expectations of the support she would get from Sam. She regularly gave him long lists of supplies she needed and details she needed him to arrange. She called Sam several times each week to clarify what she needed.

After significant prayer and a discussion with some other staff members, Sam clarified in his own mind what he was willing to do each week for that teacher and what he was not willing to do. Then he told her in a straightforward way, describing the number of phone calls he was willing to receive from her each week and which supplies the church would and would not provide for her class. He emphasized that he had other teachers and classes to support as well. He wondered if she would quit when he told her he simply could not give her the support she continually asked for, but she seemed to respond fairly well.

Sam believes that this particular teacher needs to let go of some of her perfectionism about her class. He believes that her own spiritual growth will involve adopting a somewhat more relaxed attitude and

Learning to Say No

One couple became Christians and joined our church. They were gifted, talented individuals and they got involved in everything, singing in the choir, chairing the deacons, helping with our weekly dinner for homeless people. Their life is a recipe for burnout. They are slowly learning to say no. We have all been talking to them about it.

—Karen, associate pastor in a small congregation

viewing her volunteering more as a team effort, rather than something she alone is in control of. Sam believes that when he laid out for her some limits on the support she can get, he helped move towards greater spiritual health.

Our job as congregational leaders is to promote the health of the whole community. Often that means spending time listening to people who have an issue that impacts their serving and thus also influences their relationship with God. But sometimes we simply cannot meet the needs of every volunteer in the way they think those needs should be met. Being clear about what we can and cannot do—or what we will and will not do—is one way to respond to difficult behavior.

Compulsive Behavior, Trauma Response, and Leadership

We have looked at compulsive behavior in congregational volunteers. Now we will turn briefly to look at the role of compulsive behavior in leaders. When I talked with people about burnout in their congregations, both clergy and lay people mentioned again and again the significance of the pastor or rabbi. "If the minister is compulsive about serving, it will impact the congregation." "If the pastor doesn't take days off, how will the congregation members feel the freedom to stop serving when they need to?" "If clergy don't have a private life, if they don't have boundaries around their work, what are they saying to the congregation about healthy living?"

In addition, other congregational leaders have a significant impact on the congregation's propensity for burnout. Associate pastors, nonordained pastoral staff (such as youth leaders, children's ministries coordinators, and volunteer coordinators), deacons, elders, board members, and even coffee hour and usher coordinators communicate something to the people who serve with them. Are we communicating God's call to joyful service? Or are we, by the way we model service, communicating some kind of alternative call to drudgery, fatigue, overcommitment, and neglect of family?

British physician Pamela Evans bluntly addresses congregational workaholism in her book *The Overcommitted Christian*. Her words apply to all congregation members and particularly to those of us who serve as leaders. She writes,

> People can use the process of doing church to dull their inner pain. We do well to ask ourselves from time to time:

Am I willing to examine my Christian life and service for signs of being driven by unacknowledged neediness—rather than being called and led by God? For example, is my church life lived at a workaholic pace? If so, why? What need or whose need is this meeting? Could my strong leadership be driven by a need to control (in order to feel the security lacking in childhood) rather than empowered by the Holy Spirit? Do I put so much effort into pastoral care because of an overwhelming need to be needed? Do I only sense God's love when I'm helping others? Am I only aware of his presence when I'm leading a service? Why do I go to church? Is it primarily to worship God or for some other reason?[20]

Evans's questions are a great place to start as we examine ourselves as leaders. We need to do our best to face honestly our own tendencies to compulsive behavior and the ways trauma in our own lives has driven us to unhealthy behavior. Leaders have a dual responsibility: to care for the people who serve in our areas and also to look carefully at our own lives.

If we wait until we have perfect motives, we will never do anything. But we do need to grow in understanding our motivations as leaders, to strive to move towards healthy serving that comes from our heart and our values, empowered by God's Spirit. As I consider the people in my congregation, as I look for compulsive behavior in them, I need to pay attention to my own motives and my own tendency to compulsion.

As leaders, we also need to ask ourselves whether we are promoting compulsive service in our area. This set of questions can help us consider whether we are bringing aspects of compulsiveness to our oversight of volunteers who work in our area:

- Do I watch for fatigue and discouragement in volunteers, or am I so concerned about getting the job done that I cannot see personal needs?
- Do I suggest to people that they take some time off from serving if they seem overly tired?
- After people have served for two or three years in a particular area, do I ask them to reconsider and reevaluate whether the serving is still giving them energy, or do I expect people to keep serving indefinitely?
- Is there an "honorable discharge" in my area of ministry?
- Am I open to stopping projects and ministries if keeping them going is damaging the people involved?

- Do I really believe that there is nothing we can do to earn God's love, that God's love for me and for others is abundant and unconditional?
- Do I really believe that people are called to serve from the heart, with joy?
- Do I really believe that people can find healthy places to serve, where they will grow spiritually and learn to rely on God's grace as they serve?
- What do I care about more—the spiritual growth of the people involved, accomplishing a goal, or completing a project?

We need to ask ourselves these kinds of hard questions repeatedly, because we may go into a particular season or project with our priorities clear, but as we get tired, we can revert to compulsiveness in our serving and leading.

In this area of compulsive behavior, self-examination is always the place to start and a place to return to frequently. In addition, we will sometimes need to ask people in our congregation hard questions. We may need to ask the people who serve with us: Why are you serving so hard? What personal needs lie behind all your activity? It looks to me like you only experience God's love when you are helping someone. Is that true? What can I do to help?

Bumping up against compulsive behavior teaches us over and over that we literally cannot change another person's behavior. We can look at our own tendencies to compulsion as we gently look at the ways others serve, praying that God will have mercy on all of us.

Responding to Compulsive Behavior

We have looked at patterns of compulsive behavior and response to trauma. We have seen that some people in our congregations need to be treated gently because of who they are and what they have been through. We have seen that some people need clear boundaries that lay out the kind of help they will and will not receive from others as they go about their ministry. We have seen leaders' responsibility to ask tough questions of themselves regarding their own motives for service and the way they lead in their area of ministry.

It breaks my heart to see people serving in congregations with a kind of grim determination not to quit and a depressive sense of duty. The spirit they bring to their serving violates the very purpose of what they are doing. I believe we must do everything we can to gently help people serve with glad hearts. Evans says it well:

Doing religion workaholically is an assault on the very spirituality the church promises. How can you teach life more abundant when you are working yourself to death? No church hiring committee would consider giving a job to an applicant who was an active drug abuser. Why hire an active workaholic? Same disease, same consequences, same loss of spirituality.[21]

6
IRONIES, PARADOXES, AND BALANCE

Irony
An outcome that is the opposite from what might be expected.

Paradox
Something apparently contradictory that may be true in fact.[1]

I was talking about burnout with a woman in my own congregation. She said, "I can see how burnout happens. We start off doing something because we love God. Pretty soon we are doing it because we have always done it. It is important to remember and talk about and teach about why we do things, what the real purpose is: love for God and for others."

She is so right. The very acts of service that start out as expressions of love so easily turn into obligations and responsibilities. What once came from an abundance of heart-centered caring becomes an onerous duty.

In the earlier chapters of this book, we looked at burnout in the workplace and in congregations, and we explored some of the kinds of personality differences and compulsive behavior that contribute to chronic overworking. In the preface I mentioned some of the paradoxes and ironies of burnout, and in this chapter, we will take a step back and look at them again.

As Pamela Evans writes, doing church workaholically is an assault on the very spirituality the church promises.[2] Yet people in congregations can slip into workaholic attitudes in their serving all too easily. What can we do to help people hold on to love as a motive for serving? How can we embrace wholeness and balance while calling people to the deep commitment of meaningful service?

Let us begin by laying out two ironies of burnout in congregations.

Health versus the Push to Accomplish Things

We expect our congregations to be places of health and healing, an oasis in the midst of the demands and stresses of daily life. Yet some people experience great pain in their congregations, pain that robs them of the comfort their faith could give them. Burnout is one kind of pain that goes against the very promise of congregational life.

All systems that rely on the labor of individuals, if left to themselves, will encourage burnout. The workplace, nonprofit organizations, and congregations all have a tendency to push workers towards burnout. That is because these systems have goals and leaders dedicated to meet those goals. The people working within the system very easily become the means to an end, and that end is the accomplishment of goals.

In a congregation, the goals are often lofty and energizing: rich and celebratory worship services, stimulating adult education, outreach to people who are poor and in need, care and concern for children and youth. The congregation has to keep a strong focus on its goals in order for the congregation as a whole to be healthy. Meeting those goals requires labor. The congregational system needs to get people working and keep them at it.

Hard work is necessary to make the congregation a place of refuge and rest. This is a tension, an irony, that always exists in congregations. The need for hard work pushes congregation members towards diligent service, and that kind of service can take away the sense of refuge and rest that people need. The congregation that has the goal of bringing life and health to its members may also push people towards burnout because workers are needed.

The congregation as a system will tend to call people into service for the sake of duty, which unfortunately moves so easily into workaholism. It takes effort on the part of leaders to keep priorities straight. Congregational leaders need to expend significant energy with deliberate intention in order to affirm the call to serve God with joy, from the heart, so that burnout will be less frequent.

We Start Off Well

The second irony of congregational life focuses on individuals as we enter into ministry. All too often, what starts out as loving care becomes excessive and out of balance, and we easily move towards burnout. We so often start out serving from right motivations and with healthy energy and end up somewhere we never intended to go.

Maybe this irony is clearest when we consider ordained ministers and rabbis, who are called to bring wholeness and life to their congregation through their ministry. Yet clergy get sucked into being overly busy just like everyone else. They get absorbed by what they are doing and by their goals, to the point that duty and obligation can become more powerful motivators than love and grace and health. Clergy desire to model for their congregations a life of joyful service. Yet they too often slide towards unhealthy service just like congregation members do.

One of the ordained ministers I interviewed told me that she believes that burnout is caused by taking on too much of other people's emotional reality. We overload ourselves, she believes, because we take on the emotional work of the people we care for. We begin with a lovely and appropriate kind of caring, but we move too easily into an inappropriate belief that we can fix people, provide the love for them that they never had, make up their losses for them, and so forth. We become overinvested in the well-being of others; we take on their loads. When we believe we are in some way responsible for other people's emotions, when we focus on others' "stuff" rather than our own, we move into territory that belongs to God. And we easily move towards burnout.

Sometimes we are most tempted to take on too much of other people's emotional reality when we serve with people who remind us of our family of origin. Too often, we choose places to serve where people's behavior feels familiar to us, although the settings themselves might not be at all familiar. We try to replicate our family of origin, usually out of unconscious motivations, and we will practice the dysfunctional behavior we learned there.

Taking on other people's emotional realities is just one way that healthy caring can move towards something unhealthy. Appropriate caring so easily goes over the edge into workaholism, forgetting why we are serving, or a kind of martyrdom based in duty and obligation. We are people of faith who believe in God's presence in our lives and who desire to model something wonderful to the world, yet we can slide from love to compulsion far too easily as we serve. I mentioned this irony at the beginning of this chapter when I quoted the woman in my own congregation who has noticed that as we serve, we often forget why we started serving in the first place.

The congregational system pushes volunteers towards burnout because things need to be accomplished. As individuals, we often begin serving with joy and appropriate love, and then something draws us into some form of compulsion. These are two of the ironies of congregational life.

Walking Away from Conflict

Whenever there is open conflict, people get discouraged and the departure rate from the community increases. Sometimes the parish staff become like prima donnas and refuse to share the limelight. Several times we've had talented people who are masterful at their craft but who sow seeds of division and tension. One church musician was a nationally known composer who believed that middle-class people need to be browbeaten because of their financial success. One nun ran her program in such a way as to keep herself as top dog. After these kinds of incidents, many people threw up their hands and moved on.

—Bess, member of a large congregation

Addressing the Ironies

We cannot create a faith community where all is joy and peace and rest. Some work needs to be accomplished in order for the community to exist. We cannot wait to enter into serving until our motives are completely healthy, and we cannot stop serving the moment we realize we have slid into compulsion. We are broken and flawed human beings. All we can do is try to do our best.

If we are seriously engaged in the work at hand, and if we are attempting to be as healthy and whole in our serving as possible, we will most likely find ourselves full of questions: How much sacrifice are we called to make? Jesus sacrificed himself unto death, and Christians are called to become more like Christ. Does that mean we should give of ourselves until nothing is left? What does love really look like?

Burnout Is Inevitable

Burnout is intrinsic in congregations, as is conflict. Our goal should be healthy management in the ebb and flow of congregational life. We cannot set up a burnout-free system. That's a self-defeating goal. But we can view burnout as an opportunity to help people learn what gives them joy and what blesses them.

—Mark, pastor of a small congregation

In my interviews, I was surprised at the variety of answers to this question. The answers seemed to fall into two groups. A small number of Christians I interviewed were certain that we are called to a balanced life, that our work and our service should never interfere with our family life, that all this talk about excessive sacrifice is a symptom of our culture's emphasis on self-absorption and keeping busy. One minister told me, "We tend to confuse sacrifice with a narcissistic need to be needed. We need to think we are important—a universal human need—and we in the church adopt the notion of sacrifice to enable us to feel important. If I'm always panting, running from this to that, ignoring my family, we use the language of sacrifice. But what we're really saying is that I want to be important."

Most people, however, seemed to be like me, struggling to know how to answer the questions around how to discern how much to serve. Even if they saw clearly that we are not called to sacrifice ourselves until nothing is left, they acknowledged the huge challenge they experience in knowing where to draw the line. One pastor said, "We talk about putting God first in our lives. I get a phone call from someone in need. Is that God calling me to provide care? Or is that a distraction from what I am really called to do? How do I discern? I want to keep God at the center of my life, but in practice, on a daily basis, I find it challenging to know what that looks like."

I believe the answers to these questions come from a further acceptance of paradox and irony, not from a simplistic stance that says these issues are easy to solve. We need to look deeper into our faith traditions, where we will find significant ideas that can help us.

Our Call to Service *and* to Rest

The first paradox we will look at involves a shift in the way we look at time, a shift to a view that embraces rhythm. I began to explore this view when I was assigned last year to preach on the topic of the stewardship of time. I have always viewed myself as pretty good at managing time, and I have read a fair amount on time management, so I was looking forward to imparting some practical wisdom to the congregation.

I decided I had better begin my preparation with a little biblical research to form a backdrop to the sermon. What I found in the Bible totally changed my approach to the topic. I realized how incredibly far we have come from a biblical view of time.

For us, time is linear, always moving forward in a rather relentless way. Time is all about accomplishing things. We feel driven to make the most of each moment. Most of us, I think, hope that God will bless the way we have chosen to use our time and help us maximize it.

A Biblical View of Time

The biblical view of time is both linear and rhythmical. Certainly there is the sense in the Bible that God is moving us forward in time towards a culmination or fulfillment. But in the midst of this forward movement, there is also a strong sense of rhythm. The day is marked by a rhythm of rising at daybreak, sitting down together with the family for meals, then retiring to sleep at dusk. The week is marked by a strong rhythm of six days of work and one day of rest. The rhythm of the week helps us remember that we are called to work just like God did in creating the world, but we are also called to rest like God did after creation.

The year is also marked by a rhythm of holy days that help us remember God's actions in the past. Passover reminds us of God's miracles in Egypt and Purim helps us remember Esther's faithfulness. Passover and Purim are only two of many yearly festivals described in the Old Testament and observed throughout the centuries.

In our culture, we have almost totally lost this sense of rhythm. Electricity means we do not need to watch for the sun or be aware of nature's daily rhythms. We can shop and work and engage in almost any recreational pastime seven days a week, so we have no external encouragement to observe any kind of weekly rhythm any more. In fact the increasingly popular saying "twenty-four/seven" highlights our loss of daily and weekly rhythm.

103

We have also lost much of our sense of yearly rhythm. In a pattern that is totally unnatural in the Northern Hemisphere, we can get tomatoes in January and grapefruit in August, so we have lost much of the yearly rhythm in nature that used to be reinforced by agriculture. We also defy the rhythm of the seasons by moving from north to south in the winter and then back again in the summer. Sure, we still celebrate Passover and Easter and Christmas and Hannukah, and maybe a few other holy days and national holidays each year, but that is the extent of any kind of yearly rhythm that we experience on a regular basis.

I believe this lack of rhythm is a central cause of much of the burnout people experience in our culture. We were created to live in comfortable rhythms, but we have left them aside. The psalm writers look at the movement of time as an opportunity to experience the reality of God's presence and God's blessings. They stop to thank God as they rise and as they eat and sleep each day, expressing their gratitude for God's provision of the light for work and the dark for rest and God's gift of food to eat. They experience God's special presence when they rest on the Sabbath, remembering that God is the Creator and that even God rested after creating the world. And they view the various holidays of the year as an opportunity to remember and reflect on what God has done in human history.

"Teach us to count our days that we may gain a wise heart," says the writer of Psalm 90. "Make us glad as many days as you have afflicted us," the psalmist continues. Yes, our work does matter: "Prosper for us the work of our hands," the psalm concludes.

Both work and rest matter as a part of the rhythm of time that God created for us to live in. A healthy life, a life that reflects the priorities of the Bible, will involve an acceptance of the paradox that we called to embrace both work (or service) and rest.

We Are Necessary and Superfluous

C. S. Lewis presents this reality in a memorable way at the end of the second novel in his space trilogy, *Perelandra*. In a majestic ceremony, angels make eloquent speeches about a variety of significant paradoxes. One angel says that God "has immeasurable use for each thing that is made, that His love and splendour may flow forth like a strong river which has need of a great watercourse. . . . I am infinitely necessary to you."[3]

We are infinitely necessary. Our work and service matter, Lewis is saying, because God's love is like a rush of water that needs a streambed to flow in. Truly we are God's hands and feet on earth, and we are called to reveal God's love though our actions. If we do not provide a watercourse for God's love, that love will not be able to flow into our world.

In *Perelandra*, another angel continues and says that God "has no need at all of anything that is made. . . . I am infinitely superfluous, and your love shall be like his, born neither of your need nor of my deserving, but a plain bounty."[4]

We are infinitely superfluous, Lewis says. The gift of God's love comes to us as "plain bounty," and if we do not know how to stop what we are doing and rest in that reality, we will miss something essential about who God is and who we are. We can enjoy the beauty of God's bounty and the reality that we are superfluous every day by stopping at daybreak and mealtimes and bedtime to rest for a moment in God's provision and grace. The Sabbath is a weekly manifestation of bounty and grace and abundance. Yearly festivals—Passover and Purim, Christmas and Easter—mark the ways that God has acted in history. These rhythms in time remind us that God is in control and we are not.

The Sabbath

One of the rabbis I interviewed wondered if burnout is more unusual in Jewish congregations than Christian congregations simply because of Jews' Sabbath observance. I think he might be right. I am delighted that more Christians are discovering the gift of the Sabbath. The Sabbath, I believe, is the most significant way we can act on the reality that we are called both to work and to rest, that we are infinitely necessary and infinitely superfluous.

Retreat director Tilden Edwards writes, "The Sabbath expresses the heart of the Good News, that God in Christ reveals an infinite love for us that does not depend on our works. It depends simply on our willingness for it, on our desire to turn to that Great Love with our deepest love, through all our little loves."[5] The Sabbath helps us experience that one of the most significant things we do in life is receive from God in simple dependence.

As I said in chapter 3, I have been observing a Sabbath for more than 20 years. My husband and I experienced the gift of the Sabbath when we lived in Tel Aviv, Israel, for 18 months early in our marriage. Over the years of my own Sabbath observance, I have become convinced of the deep significance of stopping my productivity every

105

week for a whole day. I experience my Sabbath more and more these days as an enacted theological statement about all life originating in God. During my six days of work, I am a steward of all that God has given me, a serious participant in God's redemption of the world. On the seventh day, I rest in the joyful reality that I am a creature, totally dependent on the One who made me, "infinitely superfluous." I experience the bountifulness of God's love and provision.

Someone told me about a Jewish tradition of praying only prayers of praise and thankfulness on the Sabbath. Six days a week, we pray for our friends in trouble, for the great needs of the world, for our own sorrows and concerns. On the seventh day, we focus on thanking God and praising God, again taking time to rest in the reality of who God is and who we are as creatures made by the Creator.

So many people tell me that they could not possibly observe a Sabbath because they have too much to do. I find I work more efficiently during the other six days because I have a rhythm of rest, but even if I did not experience any increased energy from having a regular day of rest, I would still say that taking a day off work each week reduces human arrogance and emphasizes we are dependent creatures of a loving Creator. In an article in *Christian Century*, Dorothy Bass writes, "To act as if the world cannot get along without our work for one day in seven is a startling display of pride that denies the sufficiency of our generous Maker."[6]

So much burnout seems to come from a kind of compulsion to prove something about ourselves, to keep moving in order to earn God's approval, to keep serving because exhaustion proves we are worth something. Stop! Rest! The Hebrew word for Sabbath simply means to stop. Regular patterns of stopping will teach us something significant in a way that is beyond words.

In chapter 3, I also presented some of the ways congregations can encourage Sabbath observance. The many excellent books on Sabbath keeping will answer the practical questions about what not to do and what to do on a Sabbath, and how to keep the Sabbath from becoming one more legalism. I want to reinforce here the necessity of a conscious balance between work and rest, embracing time as a source of a comfortable rhythm rather than as a harsh taskmaster. I want to encourage us to grow in seeing the rhythms of time as opportunities to stop and recognize God's abundant grace in our lives.

Our Call to Sacrifice *and* to Stewardship

The second paradox takes us deeper in the work aspects of the first paradox: When we work, how do we hold in tension our call to sacrifice and our call to be wise stewards? As I talked with people about their struggle to figure out how to serve in a way that honors God and promotes health, the most significant word I heard was "sacrifice": "We are called to be like Jesus, and Jesus modeled a life of sacrifice." Probably the most eloquent statement of this reality comes from Philippians 2:

> Let each of you look not to your own interests, but to the interests of others. Let the same mind be in you that was in Christ Jesus,
>> who, though he was in the form of God,
>>> did not regard equality with God
>>> as something to be exploited,
>> but emptied himself,
>>> taking the form of a slave,
>>> being born in human likeness.
> And being found in human form,
>>> he humbled himself
>>> and became obedient to the point of death—
>>> even death on a cross. (Phil. 2:4-8)

For most Christians, this emphasis on sacrifice has shaped their understanding of service and ministry at least to some extent. Seminary professor Virginia Wiles presents an eloquent picture of this aspect of Christian service in a baccalaureate sermon that was adapted into a magazine article:

> Ministry is exhaustion. We exhaust ourselves because of our passion for God's people and for God's world. Ministry arises out of a passionate love for the people among whom we minister. As Paul writes to the Corinthians, "I will most gladly spend and be spent for you" (2 Cor. 12:15). Spending and being spent is the nature of ministry. And it is a spending that exhausts. . . . Ministry exhausts because it arises out of our sharing of Christ's passion—Christ's passionate love for God's people and God's world. And that passionate love found its deepest expression in Christ's passionate, suffering death. Ministry exhausts because it arises out of our sharing in the passion of Christ's suffering and death.[7]

Wiles goes on to describe the sacrifices she has made so her daughters can attend college. She acknowledges that paying college tuition is a trivial example of sacrifice, but she says that the joy she has received from watching her daughters get a good education far outweighs any sense of sacrifice. She writes, "This is not masochism. Nor is it a martyr complex. . . . This is life! Not the 'meaning' of life; not the 'purpose' of life—simply life. This is what it means to 'know Christ'—to see in the cross the passion of life." She suggests that when exhaustion hits, as it inevitably will, "let us focus our eyes, our hearts, our very being on the passion of Christ, on the joy of being 'servants of Christ, stewards of the mysteries of God.'"[8]

One of the people I interviewed talked critically about the way people sacrifice themselves in service and said, "We have to remember we are not Jesus." I do agree that we are definitely not Jesus, but Paul in Philippians tells us clearly that Christians are to model ourselves after the example of Christ, an example of humility, service, and submission to the needs of others. How do we know when and where to stop serving when we do that? As I asked earlier, are we called to give ourselves until we die?

Again, I believe the answers are not simple or straightforward. Here again, embracing a paradox can help us live in the tension these questions create: We are called to be stewards at the same time we are called to live a life of sacrifice.

Stewards of Grace

A steward manages property belonging to someone else. Jesus tells a number of parables about good and bad stewards. The owner of the property in the parables wants the steward to make wise investments, balancing risk and responsibility. The owner expects the steward to give a careful accounting to the representatives sent by the owner. In a couple of the parables, the owner seems to welcome some creativity on the part of the steward.

When we survey the New Testament passages about being stewards, we see they emphasize the call to use what we have been given, to serve using our gifts, to risk with what we have been given, to step out. "Like good stewards of the manifold grace of God, serve one another with whatever gift each of you has received" (1 Pet. 4:10).

Some people who burn out need to be reminded of God's call to risk, to step out. They may have stayed too long in one place of serving, and they need to be willing to take the risk of moving on. Many people who burn out, however, need to embrace another aspect of our call to be stewards.

As stewards, we understand that everything we are and have belongs to God. Our call is to use everything—our energy, our possessions, our gifts—wisely and carefully, knowing the owner wants a return on his investment and an accounting of how we used what we were given. Remember the three original definitions of burnout that have nothing to do with people? Burnout is caused by running too much electricity through a circuit, so the circuit is destroyed. Burnout is caused by an intense fire that destroys everything in a building. Burnout in a forest happens when a forest fire is so intense that the ground is damaged, which means that the forest will come back to life extremely slowly. No owner of an electrical circuit, a building, or a forest will desire for the steward of those possessions to burn them out. Burnout causes irreparable damage. Burnout destroys the potential for rapid repair.

We know that burnout in people often causes significant growth after a period of inactivity and healing. We know that God can bring good things out of anything. The damage caused by human burnout is perhaps not as permanent as the damage to electrical circuits, buildings, and forests. However, I can still see clearly that God, as the owner of everything the steward uses, cannot possibly want us to burn out. God desires wise and careful use of all the gifts we have been given.

Yes, we are called to model ourselves after the life and ministry of Jesus Christ. His life included sacrifice. We are also called to be wise as we take care of what we have been given, carefully stewarding "the manifold grace of God." We are called to both sacrifice and stewardship. We will find spiritual health as we navigate a path that embraces them both, a path that Jesus has walked before us.

Beasts of Burden

We have used the Bible as if it was a constable's handbook—an opium-dose for keeping beasts of burden patient while they are being over-loaded.

—Charles Kingsley (1819–1874), *Letters to the Chartists 2*

The Model of Jesus: Sacrifice *and* Self-Care

Christians who tend towards compulsiveness in their service talk frequently about Jesus' model of sacrifice. They seldom talk about the way Jesus took care of himself.

I have so many questions about the way Jesus lived his life. When he went to the wedding at Cana, did he go primarily to enjoy himself, or was he already focused on the needs of the people around him and thinking about his ministry? When he ate dinner at the home of Mary and Martha, was he primarily relaxing, or was he concerned about his mission? When he went to dinners at the homes of Pharisees, did he relax and enjoy himself or was he absorbed with where he was going and what was to come?

I have read a diversity of answers to those questions, and I suppose in this life I will not know the answer to them. I believe we cannot make an argument for the necessity of pleasure and social relaxation from Jesus' model. We just do not know enough about the way he lived or his sense of purpose when he engaged in "social" activities.

We do know, however, that Jesus regularly went away for times of prayer alone. I have long been influenced by a very brief story in the first chapter of Mark. Jesus spent a day in Capernaum healing people and casting out demons. The next day, early in the morning, he rose and went to a deserted place to pray. Simon and the others came and found him and told him that everyone was searching for him. I assume the people in Capernaum wanted more healings.

Jesus had a clear sense of direction as he responded to their requests. "He answered, 'Let us go on to the neighboring towns, so that I may proclaim the message there also; for that is what I came out to do'" (Mark 1:38). People in Capernaum had more needs they wanted Jesus to meet. Jesus in effect said no to those needs because he had a sense of purpose for the day and purpose for his life. Did he get that sense of purpose from his time of prayer?

Elsewhere in the Gospels he indicates that he listens to his Father in prayer and obeys what he hears. Jesus served and gave himself for people because God directed him to do so. He was not autonomous, doing what came from within him. Neither was he compulsive about meeting every need. Long periods of prayer, a kind of prayer that involved listening, gave him his sense of direction and purpose. He learned from his prayer where to serve and where not to serve.

About 15 years ago I was asked to teach a course on the four gospels for an inner-city Bible school. My understanding of Jesus was shaped dramatically by my preparation for that class. First, I read all four gospels straight through several times. I had led many Bible studies in particular gospel passages and had studied the New Testament in seminary, but I had never looked at all four Gospels as a whole. I was surprised by several things I found.

Jesus was one of the most assertive people I have ever read about. I guess I had fallen into the habit of thinking about "gentle Jesus meek and mild," and I was stunned by the confrontational person I read about in the Gospels. Jesus was straightforward with the Jewish religious leaders, his followers, and even with some of the people he healed. In one sense he was very sensitive to the needs of people around him, but in another sense he was driven by his obedience to his Father, and the needs of people around him were secondary. He did not meet every need or live his life in response to what people expected of him. In contrast, he was very self-directed (or God-directed).

When we are exhorted in the New Testament to model ourselves after Jesus, to grow more like Jesus, we need to remember that we are following a person who gave himself for others at God's direction. He did not meet all needs. He was not "nice" to everyone. Yes, he sacrificed himself unto death. But it was God who led him there, not the desires of the people around him, or even his own desires. He experienced God's leading through extended and frequent periods of prayer.

Jesus lived a life of both sacrifice and self-care. By self-care, I mean that he knew when he needed to withdraw to pray. He knew he needed guidance from God about what to do and what not to do. He did not fall into the trap of meeting needs that were not his to meet.

Preaching Balance in Our Congregations

I love the title of Søren Kierkegaard's book, *Purity of Heart Is to Will One Thing.* Surely, single-mindedness is a characteristic of many of the most admirable people, people who have shaped our understanding of what it means to be people of faith. Single-minded devotion to God and single-minded pursuit of a lofty goal ennoble us and give us purity of heart.

How then can we talk about balance and embracing paradoxes? Is that not promoting compromise, and does compromise not dilute our inner passion and purity of heart?

I cannot imagine any individual in history or in literature who was more singleminded than Jesus Christ. Because of his devotion to God's will, he spent time in prayer, away from the crowds, listening to what his Father wanted him to do. And that gave him an ability to say no at the right times.

Using the example of Jesus, finding balance means observing the Sabbath and daily and yearly rhythms so we can remember that God is God and we are not. Finding balance means embracing the call to both sacrifice and stewardship, calls that are deeply embedded in the New Testament. Finding balance means spending time with people and time alone, so we can pray and listen. This kind of balance leads to purity of heart.

What can congregations do to help their members understand some of these paradoxes?

All congregations can promote the significance of both service *and* rest. In all our congregations, some individuals need encouragement to find a place to serve and belong, to build community for themselves and make a difference in the world. Other individuals who have long been committed to serving, need to be reminded of the significance of rhythms of rest. This teaching about service *and* rest can take place in sermons, newsletter articles, and classes. Even as we recruit for volunteer positions, we can gently communicate God's call to rest as well as work. By giving volunteers sabbaticals and by encouraging people to try new places to serve, we communicate the significance of rest. By being willing to drop programs when there are not enough volunteers to run them, we let people know that we do not value work over rest.

In congregations where the language of sacrifice has been strong and frequent, the language of stewardship can be added. In our congregations, some individuals are so oriented to sacrifice that they need to be reminded of their call to be stewards. Others are such careful stewards that they need to grow in understanding the joy of extravagant giving. Again, the language of sacrifice *and* stewardship can be used in sermons, newsletter articles, and classes. And we can model this paradox in the way we talk about volunteering and the way we treat our volunteers. Many of the practical suggestions offered earlier in this book—term limits, teamwork, sabbaticals—communicate a commitment to stewardship as well as sacrifice.

To embrace a balance of sacrifice *and* self-care, Christian congregations can draw on the model of Jesus, who drew away for prayer. Prayer retreats can be offered. Listening prayer can be modeled in worship services. Most of all, in our recruitment for volunteer positions, we can talk about the need to listen to God to be guided where to serve. We can say that a vacant position does not constitute a call to fill it. We can encourage people to try to listen to the guidance of the Holy Spirit in where and when to serve.

Christian congregations can also be careful that the Gospel is preached, that people hear the good news that nothing we can do will earn God's love for us. God's love is already there, abundant and overflowing. Many—maybe most—Christians need to grow in serving because we are loved, rather than serving in order to earn love. No one serves from pure motives. Just about every one of us has some desire for self-aggrandizement or desire to feel good about ourselves mixed in with the healthy motives for serving. A consistent message about God's unchanging and unconditional love can help all of us grow in serving more and more because we know we are loved.

Several of the writers on burnout say that serving with unconditional love, because we are unconditionally loved ourselves, seldom results in burnout. What a wonderful goal. Congregational leaders can do what they can to promote that kind of serving, knowing we are all flawed individuals who probably have not arrived there yet. God's grace abounds, calling us to serve from a heart filled with the love of God. And God's grace abounds when we have extended ourselves too far and need rest.

7
THE ONGOING CHALLENGE
OF BURNOUT

I bore you on eagle's wings and brought you to myself.
—Exod. 19:4

When I was almost finished writing this book, I got an unexpected phone call from Emma. My conversation with her helped clarify some of the key ideas I want to leave with you as this book comes to a conclusion.

Emma and I had been trying to connect for months. I do not know her well, but a mutual acquaintance told me Emma had a significant burnout story to tell me. When she called me, I could hear the tears in her voice. She said, "I just got a notice in the mail that I've been assigned to work with the two- and three-year-olds on the Sunday morning of Labor Day weekend. As soon as I read the letter, I started crying. I know I detest working with that age group, but I don't see why I'm overreacting like this."

As I asked questions, her story came out in pieces. Emma spent three years serving on the children's ministries committee at her church. With more than a hundred children to care for every Sunday morning, the committee divided up responsibilities. For most of her time on the committee, Emma served as the coordinator for the twos through kindergarten program. She was responsible for making sure enough adults were available to serve as teachers and helpers in the classrooms. Some weeks she made 30 calls in order to make sure enough people were on board. Most Sundays for three years she herself had to teach or help in a classroom because there just were not enough volunteers.

She particularly disliked working with the twos and threes. She remembers many Sundays when there were too many children and too few adults in that classroom. She also remembers that she could never get away with her family on holiday weekends, because on those weekends she always had to serve in a classroom. It was simply too hard to get enough volunteers on those difficult weekends.

After her first year on the committee, she knew she was exhausted and ready to quit. But right then the children's ministries director moved on to another job, and one of Emma's friends, Brenda, was chosen as interim director of children's ministries. Emma saw the challenges that Brenda faced and wanted to support her. After all, Brenda had no training in church work, and the job was bound to be difficult for her. So Emma decided to continue in her role for one more year.

As that second year progressed, Emma watched Brenda struggle with the workload of coordinating a children's program for so many children. Brenda had been asked to serve as interim for six to nine months, but the search committee was not able to find the right person for the job, so the months kept stretching out. At the end of Emma's second year as coordinator, she could sense the depth of her own exhaustion, but she could also see how exhausted Brenda was. She just could not leave Brenda in the lurch. So she agreed to stay on for a third year.

Emma made it through a little more than half of the third year. In March, she just could not do one more thing. She just stopped functioning. She stopped attending the children's ministries committee, coordinating the classrooms, and helping out when classes were short-staffed. She simply could not do anything more.

On that day Emma called me in tears, two years and three months had passed since she disappeared from the leadership of children's ministries. In those two years, she had continued to attend church, and she had helped in her elementary school-age daughter's Sunday school classroom a handful of times.

As Emma and I talked, I affirmed that her tears indicated unfinished business. Maybe the time is right, I told her, for some new healing or some new insights. I encouraged her to spend some time thinking, praying, and journaling about her burnout experience.

I also encouraged her to call the person in charge to say she was unwilling to volunteer even one time with twos and threes. She said she had already done that. And I told her I would be praying for her in the months and years to come, asking God to show her a place she might serve at church with joy and enthusiasm.

The Long Road towards Healing

As we have seen earlier in the book, it takes a long time to heal from burnout. Even after more than two years, Emma's emotions welled up in a powerful way as she read a letter requesting her to work on a holiday weekend with an age group she does not particularly enjoy. Since she left the children's committee, she had definitely experienced some healing. But now the time has come to look for deeper healing. Those powerful emotions indicate the presence of a wound inside her that is still raw and fresh.

When we work with volunteers in our congregations, we need to listen carefully to their stories of past service. Did they experience burnout in the past? Do some raw emotions still linger? What were the key elements that led to burnout? We will need to ask careful questions about what that volunteer wants to do and does not want to do. And we can pray with them and for them for healing from past pain.

Just a few weeks ago in my own congregation I found myself in a conversation with a woman who did a lot of the organizational work for a retreat last year. She is still bruised and raw from things that happened. She wonders if she should help with the next retreat. She has moments when she wonders if she should even attend the retreat. I tried to listen carefully to all the factors that went into her near-burnout experience, so I can watch out for her this year if she does decide to serve again.

Serving from Deep Love

In *Beating Burnout*, Minirth and the other authors argue that bitterness is often an underlying cause of burnout. When I talked with Emma, I noticed very little bitterness in her story. Occasionally she mentioned the frustration she experienced when people made decisions that made her work harder, but basically she does not blame anyone for her burnout. In this book, we have looked at other common causes of burnout, such as compulsive behavior that makes it hard to say no and congregations that encourage people to serve beyond their capacity. I did not see much of either one in Emma's story.

Emma really wanted to help her friend, Brenda, in her challenging job. Her love and care for Brenda kept her serving long beyond her own energies. Her story illustrates that sometimes we are simply caught in our desire to help. Our deeply held values will not allow us to quit, even when we know it would be better for us to do so. While we can hold this up as an example of sacrificial love, we also have to acknowledge that the exhaustion had a great price for Emma. Her congregation also ultimately paid a price, because she was no longer able to serve in any significant role.

When I am approaching the kind of exhaustion that can lead to burnout, I try to examine the forces that are keeping me hard at work. Sometimes there is compulsion and other negative motivators. But sometimes I am like Emma, trying to follow through on something because I believe in it. In these situations we need to make time to pray and listen to God's voice. We need to carefully consider God's call to both sacrifice and stewardship. We need to ask our friends or family members for their perceptions of what we should do. For me, this is the greatest challenge of serving God: responding appropriately to the exhaustion caused by love.

Using Gifts

I hope that Emma will find other places to serve, places where she can use her gifts more directly. As we talked on the phone that day, Emma told me that she is a very analytical person, a CPA who does consulting for companies who need someone to untangle complex computer and accounting problems. Her cognitive orientation and her strong problem-solving abilities were probably not very well suited for a church task involving dozens of phone calls each week to recruit volunteers. Neither were her gifts used on those Sunday mornings when she served in the classroom with very young children.

Generally we do not want our congregational volunteers to serve in positions that are identical to what they do at work. In this case, Emma should probably not serve as the church bookkeeper or the computer resource person. We want our volunteers to find service positions that round out their lives and provide balance to their work. At the same time, we want them to use their gifts.

Emma is more suited to work with older children than younger children, simply because she can relate to them on a more cognitive basis. As her daughter has gotten older, she has already found she enjoys volunteering in the classroom more than she used to. At this point, Emma has no idea where she might serve at church and use her analytical gifts. She needs to do some exploring of how she likes to use her analytical abilities in service. And she needs to grow in understanding what her other gifts might be.

Her situation points up another ongoing challenge of service. Even after we know our spiritual gifts and have a good sense of what we can contribute most effectively, we still have to make decisions about how much to place ourselves in situations that use our gifts and how much to stretch ourselves in new areas. For me, this challenge does not seem to end. Year after year I have to make decisions about what to do and what not to do, how much to go with my strengths and how much to try to grow. I see the same ongoing challenge in members of my congregation. Again, we need to make time to listen for God's guidance and the guidance of family members and friends. We need to be willing to flex and make adjustments over the years. We cannot settle the issue of where and how to serve once and for all.

Some Personal Reflections

My conversation with Emma triggered some significant thoughts about the place of exhaustion in my own life. I realized how often my values push me to keep on serving past the warning signs that I am getting very tired. And I also realized that passion to keep on serving when fatigued is a relatively new thing for me. I was ordained five years ago and received my first book contract that same year. In the past five years I have flirted with the kind of exhaustion that can lead to burnout more times than in my first 45 years all together.

To some extent I avoided burnout entirely in my first 45 years by not getting engaged in anything at a deep enough level to burn out. When I look at those years of my life, I see myself as a dabbler. I did work full time for the first four years out of college, but after that I stayed home with kids, attended seminary part time, and did various kinds of volunteering in my congregation. After seminary, I worked part time at several different teaching and editing jobs.

In fact, for 19 years of my adult life, from age 26 to 45, I moved easily from one volunteer post to another, organizing this retreat, teaching that class, helping with the youth group for six months, keeping the church books for a year. I had a pretty clear understanding that my spiritual gifts lie in teaching and administration, so I usually took on finite volunteer projects at church that usually used my gifts. When I got tired of something, I would simply quit doing it for a while. From the outside I may have looked like a model church volunteer—always willing to help with something new, willing to take on projects no one else wanted, enjoying a challenge, but not becoming so exhausted that I needed extra care or concern.

But on the inside, something was not quite right. What enabled me to quit so easily when fatigued? Part of it was a healthy sense of balance, but a larger part of it was an unhealthy sense that I really did not have anything significant to contribute anyway, so it really did not matter very much what I did. When I look back on those years, I see someone who lacked the self-confidence to believe that God would call her to anything of substance. I never cared about anything deeply enough to engage myself in a way that would risk the kind of exhaustion that causes burnout.

Now that I am serving as an associate pastor in a congregation, I am growing into the assurance that indeed God does want me to contribute something significant, and indeed God does want me to engage deeply in the ministry at hand. And I continually bump up against exhaustion.

My phone conversation with Emma brought these thoughts to the forefront, as I saw her healthy, loving desire to help her friend. She knew that what she did was making a difference. She knew that by engaging in the task, she was helping her friend. She knows now that she engaged too long for her own health, but at the time her care for her friend kept her serving.

Undoubtedly some people involved in ministry, whether as a job or as volunteers, will have an innate ability to stay in a healthy balance while engaging deeply in service. I heard from some people like that when I did my interviews. But many of us will face the ongoing, never-ending challenge of figuring out when to work and when to rest, when to sacrifice and when to steward resources, when to care for others and when to withdraw and receive nurture from God.

In the last chapter, I quoted a seminar professor who said, "Ministry is exhaustion." Yes, ministry *is* draining and tiring when we engage fully, knowing that what we are doing makes a difference, certain that indeed we do have something significant to contribute. Yet the call to be stewards and the model of Jesus tell us that we are not responsible to meet every need in the world. Everyone stops somewhere. The challenge is to hear God's voice and know when to stop.

The Energy of an Eagle

Two scripture passages have stood out for me as I have been working on this book, both of them using the image of an eagle to capture something significant about energy. The first passage comes from Isa. 40:28-31:

> Have you not known? Have you not heard?
> The Lord is the everlasting God,
>   the Creator of the ends of the earth.
> He does not faint or grow weary;
>   his understanding is unsearchable.

He gives power to the faint,
 and strengthens the powerless.
Even youths will faint and be weary,
 and the young will fall exhausted;
But those who wait for the Lord shall renew their strength,
 they shall mount up with wings like eagles,
they shall run and not be weary,
 they shall walk and not faint.

I love birds. Their flight seems so effortless, and the bird that seems to fly with the least effort is the eagle. Soaring, wheeling, catching updrafts, flapping their wings only occasionally, eagles are a perfect image of those who use energy efficiently.

I have loved this passage from Isaiah 40 for as long as I can remember. It affirms to me that God alone is the source of our energy and strength, and that something about our relationship with God will enable us to serve with the same ease and economic use of energy as an eagle.

But "waiting for the Lord" is not a phrase I relate to very well. I skip quickly over that line when I read the passage. I like to make decisions rapidly and get things done efficiently. "Waiting for the Lord" has always sounded to me like some kind of hyperspiritual attitude characterized by passivity and even laziness.

I have learned a lot about waiting in the past five years. I work in a congregation that is notoriously slow to do anything. Decisions are made slowly, plans are implemented slowly, and nothing happens quickly. In my five years as a pastor there, I have been both frustrated by the slowness and grateful for it. It is a congregation deeply committed to prayer, and I have seen a number of times that it is worth waiting for the right time to do things. When the time is right, there will be enough volunteers. When the time is right, there will be positive energy and high ownership. Since only God knows the right time, an attitude of prayerful waiting helps us discern that moment when everyone and everything will work together well.

I am convinced that some congregational burnout comes when congregational leaders move too quickly into directions that come from our own desires rather than God's leading. Some burnout comes when God is ready for us as a congregation to stop a particular ministry, but our egos will not permit us to let go of it, so we push our volunteers and ourselves to keep it going. I see the damaging effect of autonomy—trying to do things apart from God's leading—on congregational systems.

I see the same negative effect of autonomy on individuals and in my own life. I make commitments to be involved in certain ministries. I am motivated by what I believe to be God's will. I get busier, my times of prayer and reflection get shorter. I become attached to what I am doing and cannot let it go even when someone is there and available to take it off my shoulders.

Often it is the sheer exhaustion that helps me to realize the compulsion in what I am doing. I make the corrections that will help me get back on track. I schedule some longer times for prayer. I plan some time off. I sit down with my calendar and look over my commitments, making lists of things to do and things I do not need to do.

I would like to believe that after more years in ordained ministry, I will understand more easily how to maintain balance. But I am not sure that will happen. Ministry is exhaustion because we give ourselves to things that matter. In the giving we find great joy because we are using the gifts God gave us, we are working with people who help us grow in faith, and we see that what we are doing makes a difference. But ministry needs to come from God's direction and God's initiative. So the challenge remains: "waiting on the Lord" requires constant choices to listen to our exhaustion and make places in our lives to slow down.

The second passage about eagles that has encouraged me as I have written this book comes from Ps. 103:1-5:

> Bless the Lord, O my soul,
>   and all that is within me,
>   bless his holy name.
> Bless the Lord, O my soul,
>   and do not forget all his benefits—
> who forgives all your iniquity,
>   who heals all your diseases,
> who redeems your life from the Pit,
>   who crowns you with steadfast love and mercy,
> who satisfies you with good as long as you live
>   so that your youth is renewed like the eagle's.

Only God forgives and heals. Only God can redeem someone's life from the pit. Only God crowns us with love and mercy and satisfies us with good things. So often in my ministry I slide into an idolatrous belief that I can do those things for people.

As I have been writing about burnout, this passage has called me to rest in the reality that God is the one who ministers in our world.

I long for the energy of youth. I long for my life to have some eagle-like quality, some ability to soar with economy and grace as I go through my days. This passage reminds me that the greatest exhaustion happens when I take myself too seriously, viewing myself as so indispensable that I cannot rest or rely on others for help.

My conversation with Emma and these two passages that use the image of eagles helped me to realize that in my own life I need to embrace yet one more paradox. I do have something of value to offer in the world and I am called by God to engage fully in the ministry he has set out for me. I am not called to be a dabbler, doing whatever I feel like as long as it is satisfying. The kind of love that God longs for me to show in my life is a deep and costly love.

At the same time, God is the originator of all ministry, the source of all the love that we share, the one who forgives, heals, redeems, satisfies. I just cannot take myself so seriously that I put myself in the place of God; rather, I must wait on God's calling and timing. I must constantly remind myself that God is the source of all love and that God's grace fills our lives so profoundly that everything we do originates in that love and grace from God.

As a leader, I am called to help the people in my congregation understand this paradox as well. Many people sit in a pew during worship and also do some minor volunteer task because they do not believe they have anything significant to give. Many others take themselves so seriously that they are unable to rest. I need to share my journey in this area so we can grow together in healthy service.

My Prayer for You

We have heard many burnout stories. We have looked at burnout in congregations and in the workplace. We have discussed its roots in compulsive behavior, and we have explored some of the ways differences between people influence burnout. We have looked at some of the paradoxes—work and rest, sacrifice and stewardship, sacrifice and self-care—that can help us navigate a healthy path.

My prayer for this book is that congregational leaders will grow in understanding the issues around burnout so they can grow in creating communities of joy and worshipful work. I desire that our congregations be places where people's service comes from their hearts motivated by grace, where spiritual gifts are used and people grow in faith in healthy and life-giving ways, while meeting the significant needs around us.

Recently someone was telling me about a particularly successful vacation Bible school with an abundance of adult volunteers. "It was great experience for the adults," she said. "Sure it was hard work, but people were using their gifts, having fun, and getting connected to each other." That's what I long for in our congregations. Frederick Buechner writes that "the place God calls you is the place where your deep gladness and the world's deep hunger meet."[1] I long for our congregations to be places where people experience joy as they serve and meet the real needs of the world. That is what I pray for as I picture people reading this book.

NOTES

Preface

1. Abraham Heschel, *The Sabbath* (New York: Farrar, Strauss and Giroux, 1951, 1979), 6.

1   Introduction to Burnout

1. Victoria Neufeldt, editor in chief, *Webster's New World Dictionary* (New York: Simon and Schuster, Inc, 1988), 188.

2. From an interview with Robin Scherer by Carol Smith, "Step back, uncover passions to put joy back in your job," *Seattle Post-Intelligencer,* July 2, 1999, sec. C, pp. 1, 2.

3. John A. Sanford, *Ministry Burnout* (Louisville, Ky.: Westminster/John Knox Press, 1982), 3, 4.

4. Susan S. Phillips and Patricia Benner, *The Crisis of Care: Affirming and Restoring Caring Practices in the Helping Professions* (Washington, D.C.: Georgetown University Press, 1994).

5. From an interview on October 18, 2001.

6. Ibid.

7. From an interview in October 2001.

8. Pamela Evans, *The Overcommitted Christian: Serving God Without Wearing Out* (Downer's Grove, Ill.: InterVarsity Press, 2001), 172.

9. The term "worshipful work" appears in Charles Olson's book *Transforming Church Boards into Communities of Spiritual Leaders* (Bethesda, Md.: The Alban Institute, 1995). He went on to found Worshipful-Work: Center for Transforming Religious Leadership, in Kansas City, Missouri (www.worshipful-work.org).

10. Frank Minirth et al., *Beating Burnout: Balanced Living for Busy People* (New York: Inspirational Press, 1986, 1990), 44, 45.

11. Evans, *The Overcommitted Christian*, 170.

12. Ibid.

2   Workplace Burnout and Implications for Congregations

1. Quoted in Barbara Bailey Reinhold, *Toxic Work: How to Overcome Stress, Overload, and Burnout and Revitalize Your Career* (New York: Plume Books, 1997), 21.

2. Elizabeth Layman et al., "Reducing Your Risk of Burnout," *Health Care Supervisor* 15, no. 3 (March 1997): 58.

3. Jeanne Lemkau et al., "Correlates of Burnout Among Family Practice Residents," *Journal of Medical Education* 63, no. 9 (September 1988): 682.

4. Reinhold, *Toxic Work*, 9–18.

5. Ibid., 40–61.

6. Lists adapted from *The Truth About Burnout: How Organizations Cause Personal Stress and What to Do About It* by Christian Maslach and Michael P. Leiter (San Francisco: Jossey-Bass Inc., 1997); and "Take This Job and Love It: Six Ways to Beat Burnout" by Christian Maslach and Michael P. Leiter, *Psychology Today* 32, no. 5 (September/October 1999): 50–53, 78–80.

7. Judith Provost, *Work, Play and Type* (Palo Alto, Calif.: Davies-Black Publishing, 1990), 25, 26.

8. Ibid., 39, 40.

9. Frank Minirth et al., *Beating Burnout: Balanced Living for Busy People* (New York: Inspirational Press, 1986, 1990), 21.

10. From an interview with Robin Scherer by Carol Smith, "Step back, uncover passions to put joy back in your job," *Seattle Post-Intelligencer*, July 2, 1999, sec. C, pp. 1, 2.

3   What Congregations Can Do:
Identifying and Preventing Burnout

1. Pamela Evans, *The Overcommitted Christian: Serving God Without Wearing Out* (Downers Grove, Ill.: InterVarsity Press, 2001), 11.

2. Lists adapted from *The Truth About Burnout: How Organizations Cause Personal Stress and What to Do About It* by Christina Maslach and Michael P. Leiter (San Francisco: Jossey-Bass Inc., 1997); and "Take This Job and Love It: Six Ways to Beat Burnout" by Christian Maslach and Michael P. Leiter, *Psychology Today* 32, no. 5 (September/October 1999): 50–53, 78–80.

3. Malcolm Smith, *Spiritual Burnout: When Doing All You Can Isn't Enough* (Tulsa, Okla.: Pillar Books, 1995), 112.

4. Pamela Evans, *The Overcommitted Christian*, 11, 12.

5. Ibid., 13, 14.

6. Ibid., 124–31.

7. Frank Minirth et al., *Beating Burnout: Balanced Living for Busy People* (New York: Inspirational Press, 1986, 1990), 99, 100.

8. Charles M. Olsen, *Transforming Church Boards into Communities of Spiritual Leaders* (Bethesda, Md.: The Alban Institute, 1995).

9. Roberta Hestenes, *Turning Committees into Communities* (Colorado Springs: NavPress, 1991).

4   Individual Differences on the Road to Burnout

1. Don and Katie Fortune, *Discover Your God-Given Gifts* (Old Tappan, N.J.: Fleming H. Revell, 1987).

2. Anna-Maria Garden, "The Purpose of Burnout," *British Region: Association for Psychological Type Newsletter* 1, no. 6 (1990): 1, 2.

3. A good summary of the research on type and burnout can be found in "The Relationships Among Personality Type, Coping Strategies, and Burnout In Elementary Teachers," *Journal of Psychological Type* 51 (1999): 22, 23.

4. I have used a variety of books on the Enneagram, and my two friends who taught me a lot on this subject have used a lot of books, too. My favorite Enneagram books (and the favorites of my friends) are listed in the bibliography. For this section of the chapter, I relied heavily on *The Enneagram: Understanding Yourself and the Others in Your Life* by Helen Palmer (New York: HarperSanFrancisco, 1988) and *Awareness: The Key to Acceptance, Forgiveness and Growth* by Miriam Adahan (New York: Feldheim, 1994).

5. Helen Palmer, *The Enneagram in Love and Work: Understanding Your Intimate and Business Relationships* (New York: HarperSanFrancisco, 1995). Throughout the book, as Palmer describes each Enneagram type under stress, she brings into the description the possibility of movement along either arrow.

5   Compulsive Behavior

1. Frank Minirth et al., *Beating Burnout: Balanced Living for Busy People* (New York: Inspirational Press, 1997), 231.

2. Ibid., 169.

3. Ibid., 170.

4. Ibid., 168.

5. Ibid., 177–78.

6. Ibid., 184–85.

7. Ibid., 182–89.

8. Ibid., 200–204

9. *How to Beat Burnout* is published together with *Before Burnout* in one volume entitled *Beating Burnout.*

10. Ibid., 230–31.

11. Patrick Carnes, *The Betrayal Bond: Breaking Free of Exploitive Relationships* (Deerfield Beach, Fla.: Health Communications, 1997), xix.

12. Ibid., 4, 5.

13. Ibid., 6–26.

14. Judith Herman, *Trauma and Recovery* (New York: Basic Books, 1992), 34.

15. Ibid., 35. Herman is quoting from the work of Abram Kardiner describing the pathology of combat neurosis.

16. Ibid., 84.

17. Ibid., 87.

18. Arthur Paul Boers, *Never Call Them Jerks: Healthy Responses to Difficult Behavior* (Bethesda, Md.: The Alban Institute, 1999).

19. Wayne E. Oates. *The Care of Troublesome People* (Bethesda, Md.: The Alban Institute, 1999).

20. Pamela Evans, *The Overcommitted Christian: Serving God Without Wearing Out* (Downer's Grove, Ill.: InterVarsity Press, 2001), 40.

21. Ibid, 46. Evans is quoting from *Working Ourselves to Death: The High Cost of Workaholism and the Rewards of Recovery* by Diane Fassel (Lincoln, Nebr.: iUniverse, 2000).

6   Ironies, Paradoxes, and Balance

1. *Webster's New School and Office Dictionary* (New York: Faucett Crest, 1974); Victoria Neufeldt, editor in chief, *Webster's New World Dictionary* (New York: Simon and Schuster, 1988).

2. Pamela Evans, *The Overcommitted Christian: Serving God Without Wearing Out* (Downer's Grove, Ill.: InterVarsity Press, 2001), 46.

3. C. S. Lewis, *Perelandra* (New York: Macmillan, 1944), 217.

4. Ibid.

5. Tilden Edwards, *Sabbath Time* (Nashville: Upper Room Books, 1992), 91.

6. Dorothy C. Bass, "Keeping the Sabbath: Reviving a Christian Practice," *Christian Century* (January 1–8, 1997): 15.

7. Virginia Wiles, "A Passionate Exhaustion," *Perspectives* 17, no. 2 (January 2002): 24.

8. Ibid.

7   The Ongoing Challenge of Burnout

1. Frederick Buechner, *Wishful Thinking: A Theological ABC* (New York: Harper and Row, 1973), 95.

BIBLIOGRAPHY

Burnout

Evans, Pamela. *The Overcommitted Christian: Serving God Without Wearing Out.* Downer's Grove, Ill.: InterVarsity Press, 2001.
    A vivid presentation of the dangers of compulsive serving.

Maslach, Christina, and Michael P. Leiter. *The Truth About Burnout: How Organizations Cause Personal Stress and What to Do About It.* San Francisco: Jossey-Bass, 1997.
    Discusses the aspects of a workplace that make employees prone to burnout.

Minirth, Frank, et al. *Beating Burnout: Balanced Living for Busy People.* New York: Inspirational Press, 1997. (Combines two earlier books: *How to Beat Burnout* and *Before Burnout.*)
    Focuses on Christians and burnout, with particular emphasis on the effect of bitterness and obsessive-compulsive issues.

Reinhold, Barbara Bailey. *Toxic Work: How to Overcome Stress, Overload, and Burnout and Revitalize Your Career.* New York: Plume, 1997.
    Presents workplace stressors in a compelling way and makes suggestions for coping.

Sanford, John A. *Ministry Burnout.* Louisville, Ky.: Westminster/John Knox Press, 1982.
    An insightful presentation of the dangers inherent in ministry.

Sheerer, Robin. *No More Blue Mondays: Four Keys to Finding Fulfillment at Work.* Palo Alto, Calif.: Davies Black Publishing, 1999.
    An award-winning book that presents ways to make work healthier.

Swenson, Richard A. *Margin: Restoring Emotional, Physical, Financial, and Time Reserves to Overloaded Lives.* Colorado Springs: Nav Press, 1992.
    A Christian book that discusses the effect of exhaustion and overload.

Aspects of Congregational Life Related to Burnout

Boers, Arthur Paul. *Never Call Them Jerks: Healthy Responses to Difficult Behavior.* Bethesda, Md.: The Alban Institute, 1999.

Hestenes, Roberta. *Turning Committees into Communities.* Colorado Springs: NavPress, 1991.

Kise, Jane A. G., David Stark, and Sandra Krebs Hirsh. *LifeKeys.* Minneapolis: Bethany House, 1996.
    Presents five areas to explore in order to help people find a satisfying place to serve.

Oates, Wayne E. *The Care of Troublesome People.* Bethesda, Md.: The Alban Institute, 1999.

Olsen, Charles M. *Transforming Church Boards into Communities of Spiritual Leaders.* Bethesda, Md.: The Alban Institute, 1995.

Sabbath

Edwards, Tilden. *Sabbath Time.* Nashville: Upper Room Books, 1992.

Heschel, Abraham. *The Sabbath.* New York: Farrar, Strauss and Giroux, 1951, 1979.
    A classic written by a rabbi.

Muller, Wayne. *Sabbath: Restoring the Sacred Rhythm of Rest.* New York: Bantam, 1999.

Postema, Don. *Catch Your Breath: God's Invitation to Sabbath Rest.* Grand Rapids, Mich.: CRC Publications, 1997.

Trauma

Carnes, Patrick. *The Betrayal Bond: Breaking Free of Exploitive Relationships.* Deerfield Beach, Fla.: Health Communications, 1997.

Herman, Judith. *Trauma and Recovery.* New York: Basic Books, 1992.

Spiritual Gifts

Fortune, Don and Katie. *Discover Your God-Given Gifts.* Old Tappan, N.J.: Fleming H. Revell, 1987.

> Focuses on the seven gifts in Romans 12.

Wagner, C. Peter. *Your Spiritual Gifts Can Help Your Church Grow.* Ventura, Calif.: Regal Books, 1979.

> Looks at all the spiritual gifts mentioned in the New Testament plus a couple more.

Myers-Briggs Type

Baab, Lynne M. *Personality Type in Congregations: How to Work with Others More Effectively.* Bethesda, Md.: The Alban Institute: 1998.

> An overview of all the ways type can be used in congregations.

Johnson, Reginald. *Your Personality and God.* Wheaton, Ill.: Victor Books, 1988. Originally published with the title *Celebrate My Soul.*

> Describes the spiritual disciplines helpful to the different types.

Harbaugh, Gary. *God's Gifted People: Discovering Your Personality as a Gift.* Minneapolis: Augsburg Fortress, 1990.

> Looks at the ways different types serve in faith communities.

Hirsh, Sandra, and Jean Kummerow. *LifeTypes.* New York: Warner Books, 1989.

> A basic book on type

Kroeger, Otto, and Janet Thuesen. *Type Talk.* New York: Dell Publishing, 1988.

> Another basic book on type.

Myers, Isabel Briggs, with Peter B. Myers. *Gifts Differing.* Palo Alto, Calif.: Consulting Psychologists Press: 1980.

> A basic and very insightful book on type by the woman who wrote the Myers-Briggs Type Indicator.

Pearman, Roger R. *Enhancing Leadership Effectiveness through Psychological Type.* Gainesville, Fla.: Center for Applications of Psychological Type, 1999.

Pearman, Roger R., and Sarah C. Albritton. *I'm Not Crazy, I'm Just Not You.* Palo Alto, Calif.: Davies Black Publishing, 1998.

> The most recent basic book on type.

Enneagram Type

Adahan, Miriam. *Awareness.* New York: Feldheim, 1994.
  Written from an orthodox Jewish viewpoint.

Baron, Renee, and Elizabeth Wagele. *The Enneagram Made Easy.* San Francisco: HarperSanFrancisco, 1994.

———. *Are You My Type, Am I Yours?* San Francisco: HarperSanFrancisco, 1995.

Brady, Loretta. *Finding Yourself on the Enneagram.* Allen, Tex.: Thomas More, 1997.

Empereur, James. *The Enneagram and Spiritual Direction: Nine Paths to Spiritual Guidance.* New York: The Continuum Publishing Company, 1997.

Palmer, Helen. *The Enneagram in Love and Work: Understanding Your Intimate and Business Relationships.* San Francisco: HarperSanFrancisco, 1995.

———. *The Enneagram: Understanding Yourself and the Others in Your Life.* San Francisco: HarperSanFrancisco, 1988.

Riso, Don Richard. *Discovering Your Personality Type.* Boston: Houghton Mifflin Company, 1995.

———. *Enneagram Transformations: Releases and Affirmations for Healing Your Personality Type.* Boston: Houghton Mifflin Company, 1993.

———. *Understanding the Enneagram: The Practical Guide to Personality Types.* Boston: Houghton Mifflin Company, 1990.